Leave it to the Ladies

First edition

By

Hollis A. Palmer Ph.D.

Deep Roots Publications
Saratoga Springs, New York

Leave it to the Ladies

Published by
Deep Roots Publications
P.O. Box 114
Saratoga Springs, New York

Copyright 2006
By Dr. Hollis A. Palmer

Library of Congress Number 2006906628
Printed in the United States of America

ISBN 09671713-2-6

This book is dedicated to my sisters

Donna Palmer King

&

Cyndi Palmer Seifert

with deep gratitude for them not choosing the same course
as the Nolan sisters even when I gave them reasons.

Special thanks to

Heather Barrett

For refining my words so I look like
I know what happened,

And to

Jim Russo

Who once again made the book look so good.

Table of Contents

Nolan Sisters

"I don't know what poison is."

A scorecard listing the members of the Nolan family follows the story.

By Wednesday afternoon it was too late. To the exact hour it had been five days that 19 year-old John Nolan had struggled with a relentless disorder in his digestive system. What had started as vomiting and abdominal cramps had evolved until it also included diarrhea. The cramps had become so severe that all he could do in a feeble attempt for relief was lie on his side with his legs drawn up near his chest.

Each day that the symptoms persisted, Dr. Zeh, the family physician, was more perplexed by why John did not respond as would have been expected. In his mind, the doctor had prescribed all the appropriate medications. The outlook had gotten so bad that on Sunday, a priest had been called to the house to administer last rites. There had been a glimmer of optimism on the next Monday when, for a few hours, there had appeared to be a lessening of the symptoms and a reason to believe there was still hope for a recovery. However, on Tuesday John's symptoms had gotten even worse.

Over the course of his illness, John had thrashed about in pain. So violent were his actions that his aunt, who had been called in to care for John, was concerned that he would fall off the

1

bed. She allayed her fears by having his mattress pulled off the bed and laid on to the floor. Now, with even the priest having done all he could, John lay at his visitors' feet balled up in agony. He could gather some solace from the fact that he was surrounded by two of his sisters, an aunt and even a neighbor; every one present realized that John's time had come. At one o'clock in the afternoon, his labored breathing ended and John Nolan was released from his misery. Elizabeth, the youngest sister was spared the sight of her brother's death as she was working in the mill when John died.

After John passed, it would have been expected that the doctor who treated him would have signed the death certificate so the grieving family could go about arranging the burial of their only brother. The family faced a serious dilemma; Dr. Zeh refused to sign the necessary legal papers. Almost from the onslaught of John's symptoms the doctor was disturbed. One of the major contributors to the doctor's concerns was the fact that John was the fourth member of the family to die is just over six months.

Dr. Zeh was also trouble by a set of symptoms of which John did not complain. When the doctor examined John's tongue he noted that it was "heavily coated in white." Asked by Dr. Zeh, John confirmed that he had a metallic taste in his mouth – a symptom of metallic poison. From the beginning Dr. Zeh suspected arsenic poisoning and had quietly prescribed an antidote to be taken along with John's other medications. Since John had not gotten well, the doctor was certain that the medications had not been given according to the guidelines he had prescribed. It was either that the medications had not been given or someone had poisoned him a second time.

There was another set of circumstances that contributed to Dr. Zeh's suspicions. Waterford, like all small villages, had its very own unofficial rumor network. Through this communication system everyone in the community knew about Catherine's troubles.

For over two years, Catherine, the second eldest sister, had been engaged to Charles Winne. Because of her mother's poor health (she had consumption), the young couple had an understanding; Catherine would marry Winne as soon as her mother died, and a "proper" mourning period had taken place.

In the summer of 1893, without any explanation, Catherine's beau stopped visiting as often as had been his practice. In September, Winne decided he had waited long enough and, much to the surprise of Catherine, he broke off the engagement. Naturally, rumors that he was already seeing another woman started immediately. Less than a month after Catherine's break up the deaths in the Nolan house had started.

First to go was the father, Michael Nolan, who died October 23rd, 1893. Michael had worked in a forging factory having given up his farm in Stillwater eight years before. Michael Nolan had been having health issues for a year; however, his death had resulted from gastritis, a problem he had not previously experienced. Later the doctors would confirm that Michael's symptoms were very similar to John's. From the onset of his final symptoms Michael had only suffered for two days, but he had suffered severely.

Perhaps from the sudden loss of her husband or perhaps as the result of her own prolonged illness Ellen Nolan, the family matriarch, died on November 12th less than three weeks after her husband. Because it was understood that her general health was poor, no one was surprised or suspicious about Ellen's passing. That is until John died. Now, months later, there was reason to question whether Ellen's death might have been untimely.

The same night as Ellen Nolan was interred, Catherine's ex-lover, Winne married Rachel Richardson of Waterford; a choice that would later prove to not be in his best financial interest.

The feeling that the family was suffering from a set of unfortunate coincidences ended very shortly after they returned from their mother's internment. According to the family, the evening after the funeral Helena, the oldest daughter, had had a seizure. One of her siblings, which one is not clear, suggested that she be taken outside to get some fresh air. It was a damp November evening and instead of the outside air helping Helena, she was taken ill. Some accounts say she had "a chill," others suggest she also had gastritis the same as her father. In any event she died on November 23rd, 1893, exactly a month after her father and a little over a week after her mother had been interred.

There are two stories concerning Helena's illness.

According to the family, Helena had been sick for a week. In the newspapers at the time of Helena's death, it was noted she was sick for two days! Helena's obituary said she was a popular and highly respected young lady (a comment that would probably not have been used had it been Catherine who passed).

There was no reason to exhume any of the first three bodies because they had been embalmed. In the Victorian Era, one of the components of the embalming fluid was arsenic so even if Michael, Helena and possibly even Ellen had been poisoned it could not be proved.

After the first three deaths, the Nolan family consisted of: Catherine 20; John 19; Mary 17; and Elizabeth 15.

With both parents dead, Catherine enlisted the support of her aunt, Mrs. Eliza Gavin to serve as her guardian and the guardian of the three younger siblings. On November 20th, Mrs. Gavin was assigned custody of the four surviving Nolan children (Helena was still alive). That same day, Catherine, through her aunt, initiated a breach of contract suit against Winne, her former lover.

The suit was filed in county court three days before Helena died and the same day her aunt received custody. In the suit Catherine alleged that in 1889 Winne had come to her home and asked her to "keep company" with him. She went on to explain that two years later, in 1891, he had proposed marriage. The texts of the legal papers go on to say that following the proposal, Catherine had "allowed" Winne to become physically intimate. The legal papers assure the court that each time the young couple had been intimate Winne mentioned marriage. According to Catherine's account, their relationship was so well known and understood that she "went away to distant places and did things before the public with him which she otherwise would not have done with a gentleman who was not engaged to her." So serious was Catherine in her suit that she closed with the fact that she "has suffered much sorrow, humiliation, gossip, and other damages, to her person and character, and in the community, and to her peace of mind, and comfort as well as her future happiness, all be her damages as she verily believes to the extent of TEN THOUSAND DOLLARS." [The bold was in the original text.]

Although not all the characteristics were positive, the

Nolan children had several distinguishing features. All five of the offspring were thin and looked significantly younger than their actual age. John, who was six feet tall, weighed only 135 pounds. The newspapers described the girls, including Catherine, as looking at least two years younger than their actual age. Despite their Irish extraction the children did not have red hair. The girls also lacked what would be considered by today's standards as sophistication. Their simple understandings were demonstrated by the way they, over the period between the onset of John's illness and the close to the trial that followed, would continuously alter their stories. It was as if they were trying to please whatever audience was present. The changes they made were not just the fine details but also on major points.

Another interesting characteristic of the siblings was their diet. In the months that followed the passing of the parents, the four children ate what they wanted without regard to nourishment. They did, however, honor the Catholic doctrine that required the eating of fish on Fridays.

The Plot Thickens

Understanding his responsibilities in a case where there were indications of poisoning, immediately upon John's death Dr. Zeh went to Coroner Stubbs to express his concerns. Zeh related his suspicions and asked Stubbs to investigate. Hearing the extent of Dr. Zeh's suspicions and, knowing that the doctor was not an alarmist, Stubbs believed he would need to convene a coroner's jury (today made part of the grand jury system). The Victorian Era was a time when it was more common for people to die in street and bar fights or along the canals by muggings. In cases where there was a suspicious death, a coroner's jury was convened to try to determine the cause of death and if a homicide was ultimately suspected, the juries would often name a suspect. A hearing before a coroner's jury was not a criminal trial in that they could not actually convict anyone.

John Nolan's death occurred before photography was commonly admitted as evidence in trials. To be sure that there were independent witnesses, members of a coroner's jury were expected to examine the body. Since the scene might provide indications as to the cause death, if possible, the coroner's jury as

5

a group would visit the scene of the death. Like a grand jury today, coroner's juries could hear testimony from witnesses. The testimony before a coroner's jury was recorded by a stenographer, but not by a court reporter. Following the inquiry, witnesses were provided copies of their testimony to review and they were allowed to make corrections if they felt they were needed. When a witness felt the statement reflected what they meant they were expected to sign a copy.

Based on what Zeh related, Stubbs assumed that an autopsy would be required. While he made the necessary medical arrangements, he instructed Deputy Sheriff Alvin Collins to gather twelve men to serve on the coroner's jury. Stubbs instructed Collins that he would meet the men at the Nolan's house.

Waterford, because it is at the junction of the Erie Canal, Champlain Canal and Hudson River, had a transient economy during the Victorian Era. Because so many people passed through, there were always people who lived according to questionable values. Even within this population a murder, or even an alleged one, was not something that occurred every day. The men Collins chose to be on the coroner's jury knew they were in a unique position to become involved in an event the town would talk about for years.

At the Nolan House

Coroner Stubbs arrived at the Nolan's small home at about 3:00; two hours after John's death. There he was met by twelve men who were standing around in front of the house talking among themselves. Unfortunately, counted in the twelve men was Deputy Collins. It seems that, when Collins gathered the coroner's jury, as instructed, he elected to incorporate himself in the twelve men required. Collins' inclusion meant that one of the persons involved in the investigation was also serving in judgment.

Inside the Nolan house, in addition to John's body, were his three surviving sisters and an aunt. The aunt, Mrs. Gavin, was a sister of the father, Michael Nolan, who came when she heard John "took sick." The gathering of a group of men, few if any of whom were known to the family, just outside their fence, sent waves of caution and concern through the Nolan women.

While the other men waited outside the family's fence,

Stubbs and Collins went to the front door. They knocked. When asked why they were there, they explained their purpose. They were denied admission to the house by the women inside. Stubbs and Collins tried to open the door but, because it was locked from the inside, the door would not budge. Realizing that nothing was going to happen as long as they stayed at the door, the two men walked into the side yard looking for a second way to enter. While they were in the yard the two men encountered Mrs. Gavin, who had come out the back door to confront them. Collins explained to Mrs. Gavin that they were at the house to investigate John's death, adding that it was necessary for a coroner's jury to see the body where it lay. During the discussion that ensued, Mrs. Gavin made it clear she had no intention of letting any of the men into the house.

Either Mary or Elizabeth, no one was sure which of the two younger sisters it was, was at an open window. The nervous young girl asked her aunt, "Shall we open the door?"

The aunt responded with a plain, unconditional, "No."

To his credit, Deputy Collins tried to mellow the situation telling the older woman, in a non-confrontational tone, that she "was doing wrong." He went on to explain that the men outside the gate would have to come in the house. Again she refused.

While Collin's continued to try to reason with the aunt, Coroner Stubbs decided to take matters into his own hands. Stubbs climbed in one of the windows. He immediately went to the front door and after unlatching it, he called for all the other men to enter. With the door finally open, the men followed Stubbs' request and plowed into the living room.

The men's entry into the house was so disturbing to the sensitive Catherine that, minutes after the jury came through the door, she had a seizure on the living room floor.

The members of the jury had to climb to the stairs to the second floor to get to John's bedroom. There the men witnessed the body lying on the thin mattress placed on the floor. John was on his side, his legs were drawn up and his arms were across the chest indicating the pain that had accompanied his death. The skin was still clammy and grayish in color.

After witnessing the agonizing position John had assumed

prior to death and the seeing the incriminating way the members of the family behaved, those in the coroner's jury were justifiably apprehensive about ruling on the cause of death. To relieve their anxiety the jury members decided that before a verdict could be rendered they needed to hold a full inquest. To keep things official, before the members of the jury left the front of the house, they officially ordered that an autopsy be performed.

The coroner instructed that John's body be taken out of the house and placed on a wagon bound for Dr. Shearer's office for examination. Wisely, as the physician who had treated John, Dr. Zeh was not to be the lead doctor for the autopsy. To be sure that his concerns were checked, Dr. Zeh would assist Dr. Shearer. There would not be a conflict of interest on this topic.

Autopsy

Dr. Shearer was an experienced physician having practiced medicine for 15 years in Waterford. In his initial request, Coroner Stubbs directed Shearer to examine John's remains for signs of arsenic poison. Additionally, the internal organs, where arsenic was known to collect, were to be removed and placed in glass canning jars to be taken to Professor Perkins of Union College the following day.

Perkins, a chemist, was considered one of the first experts on forensic medicine having been involved in over forty other cases where poison was suspected. In the course of examining John's organs, Perkins found five grains of arsenic in the stomach, with additional grains of arsenic found in the liver and other organs.

It was in the delivery of John's body parts to Perkins that the defense would gather even more momentum. Since it might cause some concern to just ship human organs in glass jars, Stubbs needed someone responsible to actually transport the jars from Waterford to Schenectady. He selected Deputy Collins to serve as the currier. As a member of the coroner's jury, an investigator and now a currier, the defense was gaining more reasons to question the mixture of roles Collins was playing in this one investigation.

When Dr. Zeh reported his suspicions about John's death to coroner Stubbs he had added an interesting anecdote. It seems that in the days while John was suffering, Zeh was concerned about the possibility of poison. To remove his apprehension, Zeh had instructed Elizabeth, the youngest daughter, to save any vomit in clear glass jars. So there would not be an excuse for not doing as requested, Zeh had even provided the jars. On later visits, when he asked her for the containers, he discovered that she had refused to save the contents of the night pan and, in fact, had buried the waste in the backyard. [Note: this was before the days of indoor toilets in humble homes.] When she was questioned about why she had not done as requested, Elizabeth first told Dr. Zeh that she had not saved the waste because the priest had said it was against the sacraments. She would change her reason later.

Based on Zeh's information, Stubbs had questioned Elizabeth concerning where in the backyard she had buried the waste. In addition to the body parts, Stubbs had some men remove the earth where Elizabeth said she buried the waste. The amount of earth removed from this site was the size of a wash pan. Stubbs had the men take a second sample of earth from another part of the yard to use for comparison. The samples of earth, along with the organs, were sent to Professor Perkins. Perkins would discover another grain of arsenic in the sample where John's waste had been buried and no arsenic would be found in the other sample of earth from the same backyard.

The parts of the story that do not change

As was his practice, on Friday June 8, 1894, John came home for his lunch (the family called it dinner). The simple meal consisted of bread, fish and tea. From the first time the story was told until the last, there was a consistent point about the table. According to all the statements, when John arrived home for lunch Elizabeth had put four place settings on the table. There was also agreement on the preparation of the fish dinner. Everyone agreed that it had been prepared by Catherine and was served family style; all the fish was on a common platter, placed in the center of the table. Everyone also agreed that Catherine never joined her brother and sisters at the table.

Each person took a section of the fish and broke off chunks from the same loaf of bread. It was in the drinking of the tea that there was a difference in what people consumed. John was the only member of the family who consistently used sugar in his tea.

Elizabeth would use sugar if there was not any milk; however, this day there was milk to add to the tea. It appeared Elizabeth was just helping when she served John his cup of tea. Elizabeth and Mary, the two sisters at the table, said that he added some sugar himself; however, there was some discussion as to whether Catherine had placed sugar in the empty cup before she went outside.

Catherine elected not to join her brother and two sisters for their midday meal; choosing instead to spend the time in the family garden. After her brother and sisters had eaten, and after John had gone back to work, Catherine came in to the kitchen and ate her lunch by herself.

Since John had to walk from the mill and back, he only had approximately 15 minutes to actually sit at the table for his lunch. Mary, the middle surviving sister, would later remark that when John left the house to return to the mill he was whistling and singing.

The story changes

The reports of what Catherine did when she came in from the garden changed each time a story was told. When the sisters, Mary and Elizabeth, were first questioned, they said that after John left for work they had placed the dirty dishes on the stove. They went on to explain that when Catherine came in she had taken out a clean cup and sat at the fourth table setting to eat her lunch. After the inquest, the story changed to Catherine having washed the dishes before sitting down for her own lunch. At the trial that would follow, Mary, the only sister to testify, said Catherine had eaten her lunch on John's dirty dishes and that she drank from his dirty cup. There was no need for Catherine use dirty dishes as there was a fourth place setting on the table.

After lunch John returned to work arriving at his usual time. As the afternoon progressed, he became increasingly thirsty. Since this was long before the days of bottled water, John relieved his thirst by drinking water from the tap at the mill. John was able to stay for his entire shift; however, at some time during the afternoon, he became so sick that he started to vomit.

When his shift was over, John returned home arriving about 6:00 pm. When he got to the house Catherine was sitting on the front stoop with David Doughty. (Their relationship is not clear; however, he was not a member of the family.) As he handed over ten dollars to pay for the family's food and bills, John told his sister he was not feeling well. According to Catherine, John attributed his illness to drinking the water at the mill. Doughty added that while John was still on the porch he told him that he had been sick all afternoon.

John was nineteen, an orphan, single and brash; no simple illness was going to keep him in on a Friday night. John left the house approximately a half hour after he had gotten home from his shift. He spent the next four and a half hours visiting at least two different taverns in Waterford.

In the tavern owned by Michael Curtin, John had two drinks, both comprised of whiskey. After 8:00 p.m. John went to Richard Costigan's bar where he had several more drinks. Because John threw-up several times at Costigan's, the bartender did not think he was drunk when he left a little after 11:00 p.m. It should be noted that the bartenders from each place admitted to drinking from the same bottles. Later it would be established that no one else that was out in the same bars that evening had similar symptoms. A reasonable assertion can be made that whatever John consumed that carried the poison it was not from anything in any of the taverns. John was also the only person at the mill who exhibited the symptoms.

The front door was locked when John got home around 11:30 p.m. He knocked until his sister Mary got up and let him in. It was Mary's feeling that John acted as though he was drunk. She said that he was so weary that he sat down in a rocking chair where he fell asleep.

On Saturday morning when John awoke, he was feeling even worse. What had started out as stomach issues had expanded to his intestines and now included diarrhea.

Richard Costigan, one of the bartenders who had served John the previous night, was so concerned about John's health that on Saturday he dropped by the family's home to check on him. There is no record that Costigan and John were friends, so the bartender's visit is an indication of how serious his concerns were for a patron. Costigan found John sitting at the kitchen table looking pale and very ill. Costigan's comment to John was that he "ought to have a doctor." John responded to the bartender that he believed that he would recover without the help of a physician.

That same Saturday evening, John Costin, a friend of John's, dropped by the Nolan house. Costin had heard that John was not well and wanted to see for himself how his friend was faring. By this time John had been moved upstairs to his own bedroom. After Costin sat with his nauseous friend for a while, he came down and asked Catherine what was making John so ill. Catherine told Costin that an unidentified doctor said John had diabetes. Over the course of the next two days, Catherine would tell at least two other people that a doctor had concluded that John was diagnosed with diabetes. No doctor ever was found who made such a diagnosis.

As Saturday progressed, John's sisters discussed their options. They decided on a two pronged solution. First they would summon their Aunt Eliza, their guardian and the one who had cared for their father and sister the previous fall. John's sisters also decided to seek medical assistance from Dr. Zeh. Since hospitals were rare and medical insurance for laborers nonexistent, John like others, was treated at home.

Dr. Zeh came by shortly after being called. From the time he arrived on Saturday until John's death on Wednesday, Dr. Zeh visited the house at least once each day, usually more than once. When John showed no signs of improving by Monday, Dr. Zeh decided he wanted a second opinion. Zeh contract Dr. Shearer who agreed to join him when went to the Nolan's house to check on his patient.

Treatment

Zeh's treatment began with a prescription for sub-nitrate of bismuth bicarbonates combined with carbonic acid and acacia. This concoction was made consumable by mixing it with peppermint water. At the time this was the standard treatment to relieve the symptoms John exhibited. [None of these products contained any arsenic.] When John did not respond to the medication as expected and upon seeing his tongue, Dr. Zeh added an antidote for arsenic poison to the treatment. As the days progressed, there was no evidence that John was responding to medication or the antidote. Dr. Zeh began to believe that John was not receiving the antidote according to the timelines he prescribed.

As already noted, Elizabeth did not save the waste, but her reasons for defying the doctor changed over the course of the investigation. At first she told people that a priest had told her that, as a Catholic, she had to bury the waste. Later she would say that that her reason was that the family had been told to bury waste of a sick person long before by a nurse.

From his lunch on Friday June 8th until his death on Wednesday the 13th, everything John Nolan ate while at home was prepared by his sister Catherine. Most of his meals were served to him by either his aunt or his youngest sister, Elizabeth. There is no record of his having eaten while he was out the evening of June 8th; however, he was absent for over four hours and may have had some snacks. There is an equal chance that because he was already sick he did not have any food that evening.

During the period of his illness, the only days that John had cooked food was on Friday and Tuesday. On Friday he had the meal of fish and bread. On Tuesday he had what was basically a broth. The foods he consumed on the other days were raw. The record shows that when John realized how sick he was on Saturday, he set out to make himself a mixture that would either make him sicker or help him get well. On Saturday morning he sent his sister to buy ten cents worth of whiskey. To the whiskey he added four raw eggs. To flush the eggs down he had a bottle of soda water and five bananas topped off with an orange. He finished the delectable meal off with some coconut straight from the shell. Later that evening he had a seidlitz [sic] powder was added to reduce the symptoms.

Investigation

The decision by the coroner's jury that it needed more information before rendering a verdict allowed time for a more comprehensive investigation. Working off the assumption that John's death was the result of the administration of poison, there were the standard questions of access, opportunity and motive that required investigation. In this case:

- Who had access to poison? And where had they purchased it?
- Who had an opportunity to administer the poison? And how had it been administered?
- Was there a motive for poisoning John? Assuming there was a motive, who held that motive?
- Did anyone try to prevent John from getting help?

Any investigation starts with the people closest to the victim.

Mrs. Gavin was claiming that in her function as nurse she had fed John his last sips of broth; however, she was not present during the onset of his symptoms. Therefore, if she was not present on Friday, how had John initially gotten sick (poisoned)? Although not ruled out as a suspect, Mrs. Gavin was not the logical choice.

His middle sister, Mary, had been nervous but did not appear to have been involved in the preparation or serving of John's meals. There was little reason to suspect her.

Elizabeth had set the table and served the tea. She had also refused to save John's waste products. There were reasons to consider her as a candidate.

Catherine had prepared John's meals and had served him whenever he was not served by his aunt. Catherine had also been conveniently absent from the table for John's last regular meal. Additionally, everyone knew of Catherine's personal problems.

During the Victorian Era, sanitation was nowhere near the level it is today. People across economic levels were annoyed by lice, bedbugs, and rodents. To eliminate these nuisances, drug stores were permitted to sell poisons over the counter. To receive a supply of poison for a home or business, a person merely had to go to an apothecary. The druggist would measure out the poison, wrap it in paper and label it as a poison. The buyer had to give a reason they wanted the poison (to kill mice) then they signed the poison book.

Given that there was time for an investigation Deputy Collins went to the local drug stores to see if any of the people in the family had purchased arsenic. Examining the poison book at John Higgins & Company drug store, it was learned that on October 14th, 1893, a Sarah Nolan had purchased 100 grains of arsenic. This was less than two weeks before the father had died. The problem was that no one in the Nolan family was named Sarah. Upon questioning George Cole, the druggist at Higgins's drugstore, he identified "Sarah" as one of Michael Nolan's oldest two daughters; he was not sure which one. The problem was that the two oldest girls were Helena, who died a month later and Catherine.

The poison book in another drugstore showed that a Lena Nolan had purchased arsenic "for rats" on November 11th, 1893. This was two days before the mother's death and twelve days before Helena's death. Again there was no Lena in the family but it was soon learned that Lena was the name that Helena went by. In this case the druggist was not sure if the person who purchased the poison was Helena or Catherine but he was certain it was one of Michael Nolan's two oldest girls.

An examination of the poison book at Spaulding's Drug Store failed to indicate a sale; however, Bert Shaw, the clerk, said that one of the daughters of Michael Nolan had been in the store with Winne and while she was there she tried to buy poison "to kill a dog." Shaw was not sure if the incident was in late September or early October 1893, but he was sure it was in the early fall. The reason he had not had her sign the book was that he had not sold her the arsenic she had requested. Instead Shaw had substituted "sugar of milk." Shaw said it was not his practice to substitute a harmless chemical for a poison but that he had in this case because of the way the girl acted.

Discussing the case with Mrs. Currier, a neighbor of the Nolans, it was learned that Catherine never went by her given name. For reasons that no one stated Catherine was usually called Sadie but on occasion she was called Sarah.

The Inquest

Even while the autopsy was going on it was understood that it would take time for Professor Perkins to complete his chemical analysis. Rather than waste the time required for the analysis, the coroner's jury conferred an inquest and began collecting evidence. A coroner's inquest, such as the one in the Nolan affair, often included the questioning of witnesses. The inquiry would be held on three different dates with the final date being July 13, one month after John's death. The final date included the testimony of Professor Perkins.

The inquest discovered evidence regarding who had purchased poison, the history of the deaths in the family, who had prepared and served the food John consumed. There was also testimony as to the issue between Charles Winne and Catherine.

At the inquest there were two very different tales regarding the clearing of the table. According to Mary and Elizabeth, when they finished lunch they cleared the table and placed the dirty dishes on the stove. They told how when Catherine came in she took a clean cup from the cupboard then ate her lunch at the fourth place setting. In sharp contrast, Catherine said that when she came in the dishes were all still on the table and she ate from John's dirty plate. She added that she also drank her tea from his cup. Perhaps because they did not want to interfere with, or tip their hand for the trial, Catherine was never asked, nor did she explain, why she did not use the clean place setting.

Mary and Elizabeth both told the coroner's jury that Helena had sometimes gone by the name Lena; however, Mary added that all the girls used the name Lena on occasion. If Mary was telling the truth then the purchase of poison in November could have been made by Catherine or, for that matter, any of the sisters.

Catherine told the coroner's jury that on the Saturday that John was taken ill she had gone for Dr. Peckham, a Cohoes doctor who had treated her father. She testified that he was not home so she went even farther, to Green Island, in search of a doctor. Catherine claimed she was not able to get a doctor to come from Green Island. When she got home the family finally elected to seek help locally in the person of Dr. Zeh. There was no explanation why Catherine would have felt the necessity of going so far when there were several doctors in Waterford.

The other new piece of information that came out at the hearing was the existence of several life insurance policies. Michael Nolan was insured for $600; Ellen (the mother) had no insurance; Helena had a policy for $200 with a deducible. John had a complicated two part policy that, if it were to pay in full, would have a total benefit of just over $400. Michael's policy, which was older, was to be paid jointly to Helena and Catherine. Helena's policy for $186 had been paid to Catherine.

On July 13th, Perkins testified as to the existence of arsenic in John's organs, in sufficient quantity to kill. The chemist's testimony was enough for the coroner's jury to be convinced that there had been a murder. The jury declared John's death the result of arsenic and held that there was sufficient evidence that Catherine and Elizabeth should be held over for the grand jury. The two were arrested that day.

During the inquest Deputy Collins had complicated his objectivity in the case. While the coroner's jury was hearing the testimony of several witnesses, Collins, as the deputy sheriff, would often be required to go out into the community to gather someone who was to testify later. This meant he had missed the testimony that was given while he was absent; an issue the defense would use later.

The day following their arrest, Catherine and Elizabeth were taken by train to the county jail in Ballston Spa. On the trip they were accompanied by Deputy Collins. While the sisters were on the train, Collins advised Catherine that she had better tell everything she knew about the matter, reminding her that she had been charged with the murder of her brother. Catherine was cool and responded that if John was poisoned, "someone else done it." Undaunted, Collins elaborated saying that there was evidence that she had tried to "buy poison in Cohoes." Catherine responded to his accusation, "I don't know what poison is." Under Collins' continued prodding she explained, "There was never any [poison] in the house." Their conversations added one more way he was involved in the case.

It was July when the sisters arrived in Ballston Spa. A grand jury heard evidence in October and filed formal charges against both sisters for murder in the first degree.

For nine months the two sisters would be remain in the county jail.

Although Mrs. Gavin had been given legal custody of the Nolan children the previous November, she had continued to live in Stillwater. The reality was that Catherine had taken care of the family. With Catherine in jail there was no one to officially care for seventeen year-old Mary. She was remanded to the county home.

Mary was released a short time later and went to Stillwater where she stayed with her aunt, Mrs. Gavin.

There is an unanswered question as to why Elizabeth was charged and not Mary. Elizabeth's complicity, if there was a murder and if she did assist, seems to have been two different acts. At the lunch in June she was the person who actually served John his tea. If there had been arsenic in the cup, and not the sugar bowl, she could have either placed it there or at the least she might have noticed that it was in there. Also, as a possible accomplice, her refusal to save the waste; even when directed to do so by the doctor would have caused some concern. In addition to her actions, Elizabeth had changed the details of her story more than Mary between the incident and the formal inquiry.

Media Coverage

From the very first reports of a possible fratricide, this story received considerable coverage in the media. All the regional newspapers covered the story. The amount of space and the page on which it was carried varied considerably based on the newspaper's proximity to Waterford. In addition to the extensive local coverage, at the time of John's death and during the inquiry that followed *The New York Times* carried two articles about the case. The *Times* would carry a two additional stories and an editorial during the trial.

The New York World, based in New York City was what would be considered a tabloid. The *World* could be counted on to feature stories about the most outlandish incidents and trials that were happening throughout the country. The *World* virtually always implied that the person on trial was guilty. In examining their stories one is left with the impression that they focused on the bizarre and threatening scaring their readers into feeling totally unsafe.

The editorial staff at the *World* understood that the trial of the Nolans was the kind of account that was their specialty. It was to be the trial of sisters accused of killing their brother with implications that they may have also been involved in the deaths of other members of the family. Based on its regular stories it was obvious that coverage of this trial would push sales. The newspaper assigned Mrs. McQuirk to cover the story. In fairness, the stories the *World* carried about the trial were among the more interesting reports.

There was one fundamental difference for the *World's* coverage of this one case. For once the *World* changed its usual perspective and brazenly took the side of the Nolan sisters.

The Trial

Going into the trial, the prosecution acknowledged that it had a case based almost exclusively on circumstantial evidence. The prosecution admitted that it was further hindered by the reality that most of the witnesses to the events up to John's death were members of the family of the accused. As mentioned in their own opening statement, the prosecution would have no witness who would testify that he or she had seen Catherine placing poison in the food or drinks consumed by John. What the prosecution did not mention was that those looking for reasonable doubt would be facilitated by the fact that Catherine's given name did not even appear in the drug store records. What did appear were names that she had been known to have used.

To understand why (with the obvious weaknesses in the case) the prosecution felt they had to go forward, one only needs to look at the sequence of events which were loaded with interesting, almost unexplainable, coincidences.

Sequence of events
1893

- During the summer Charles Winne stopped seeing Catherine on a regular basis – he continued to see her occasionally until two weeks before her father's death.
- September or early October, one of the two older Nolan girls visited the Spaulding's Drug Store where she attempted to purchase poison "to kill a dog." The drug store clerk supplanted the arsenic with a harmless chemical.
- October 8 – Charles Winne has waited long enough and officially breaks off his engagement to Catherine.
- October 14 – "Sarah" Nolan purchased 100 grains of arsenic at Higgins Drug Store "to kill rats."
- October 23 – the Nolans' father, Michael, died after suffering from gastritis for two days. His symptoms were

similar to John's.

- November 11 – "Lena" Nolan purchased three cents worth of poison "to kill rats."
- November 12 – Ellen Nolan died possibly of consumption.
- November 15 – Ellen Nolan is interred.
- November 15 – According to one witness, Helena Nolan has a seizure following her mother's funeral.
- November 15 – Charles Winnie marries
- November 20 – Catherine sues Charles
- November 23 – Helena Nolan dies after suffering for two days.

1894

- June 8, 1894 –John has lunch then returns to the mill where he becomes sick during the afternoon.
- June 12 – 13 John told Dr. Zeh that he had nothing to drink the night before; Catherine said she gave John a drink of lime water.
- June 13 – John has a last meal of beef tea and dies within an hour.
- June 29 – Catherine went to see Cole at his drugstore and asked him to contradict what he had testified to before the coroner's jury; that "Sarah" Nolan purchased arsenic. This was not in the previous testimony.

The judge in the trial was Charles Landon, one of the most respected Jurists in the area. He had presided in many contentious trials including the first trial of Jesse Billings. He was from Schenectady and served on the board of Union College.

The prosecution and the defense were lead by some of the more notable attorneys in the area. District Attorney John Pierson of Saratoga and his Assistant District Attorney H. E. McKnight of Ballston Spa headed the prosecution's team. Because of the significance of the case the venerable Judge Jesse L'Amoreaux was brought in to assist the prosecution. L'Amoreaux would not be expected to deal with the pressure of direct or cross examination but would use his oratorical skills in the opening and closing arguments. The final member of the team was Charles Clapp, a young attorney.

The local press was quick to point out that Pierson's salary had just been raised by sixty-six percent. Yet, for this, his first big trial since the increase, he needed to spend even more taxpayer dollars for L'Amoreaux's support.

The Nolan sisters were without funds so their attorneys were appointed by the county. Normally, the courts were careful to only appoint attorneys who were residents of the county to serve as defense counsel. The court made an exception in this case. The Nolans were allowed to use Charles Keach. Keach had represented the family in the past. When Judge Landon learned that the prosecution had added L'Amoreaux and Clapp, he allowed Keach to be joined by Irving Wiswall, an attorney from Ballston Spa.

From the initiation of the law lawsuit against Charles Winne, Catherine had been represented by C. E. Keach, a young attorney from Lansingburg. The experienced court reporters sent to follow the trial describe Keach as a legal technocrat. He seemed to live to make objections, never conceding a point; and fighting to keep everything incriminating from being heard by the jury. One of the key issues Keach wanted kept out of the record was any mention of the deaths of the other three Nolan family members who had died in the preceding eight months. In Keach's mind, since Catherine was not charged in the other family members' deaths, those deaths should not be revealed. It is obvious that if Keach had a sense of justice, it was only as he saw it.

Initially, the prosecution planned to try the two sisters at the same trial. One of Keach's first motions was for separate trials. He knew that the more evidence a jury heard, the more likely a conviction. If the sisters were tried together there would be more incrimination, such as Elizabeth's destroying the waste and Catherine's possible purchase of poison. With separate trials, these topics would only be included in the trial of the sister accused. He wanted to avoid the appearance of a conspiracy.

Landon ruled in favor of the defense setting two separate trials, one to immediately follow the other. Since Elizabeth was only 15 at the time of the trial, if the judge had not ruled for separate trial there would have been the issue of an adult (Catherine) being tried with a youthful offender (Elizabeth). The prosecution was able to decide which trial would go first and elected to start with the trial of Catherine.

Keach's meticulous and detailed questioning resulted in it taking over a day just to select a jury. In 1895, the selection of a jury often took only a few minutes and rarely over two hours. To those present, it appeared that at even at this early stage of the trial Keach's attitude was wearing on the judge.

There were only 38 potential jurors called, twelve served. Eleven were put aside by the court; primarily because they said they would not convict on circumstantial evidence. Eleven were challenged by the defense while only four were challenged by the prosecution. It is worthy of note that none of the jurors lived in Waterford, where the Nolans resided nor was there a juror from Stillwater, the family's previous residence.

No sooner was the jury sworn in than the prosecution raised a difficult matter relating to one of their key witnesses. During the time the girls were in custody, Mrs. Gavin's tuberculosis had gotten worse. There was a serious concern as to her ability to travel to Ballston, let alone testify in a courtroom. The prosecution asked Judge Landon to allow both counsels to go the Gavin's residence and take a deposition which would later be admitted into evidence. Keach would have nothing to do with such an arrangement. It appears he either wanted to draw on the sympathy the testimony of a dying woman would have on the jury or to be able to use her ministration of John's last meal as a reason for reasonable doubt. Mediator that he was, Landon ordered that a physician be sent to Stillwater to accompany Mrs. Gavin back to Ballston where she would be put up in the Hayner House (hotel). He deferred ruling on how her testimony would be given until the doctor returned.

The remainder of the first day of the actual trial was spent on the testimony of Coroner Stubbs, Dr. Zeh, and Deputy Collins. These men's testimonies were to prove a death, present the behavior of the family when the coroner's jury had gone to the house; and the symptoms John had exhibited.

Through the cross-examination of Collins, the defense started to build their case by attacking his various roles. It was the defense's contention that Collins was biased from the beginning and his overlapping roles meant that Catherine's explanations were never looked at objectively. Keach would describe the treatment of Catherine by Collins as "persecution rather than prosecution."

Although the prosecution assumed that Catherine would not testify in her own defense, they wanted to use her own words against her. Since Stubbs was the coroner who lead the inquest, the prosecution requested him to read the testimony she had given in front of the coroner's jury to the jury in her trial. Keach objected, claiming that she had not been provided counsel when she testified. Under questioning by Landon, it was learned that Keach had attended the coroner's jury on behalf of the Nolans. Although he had not officially been appointed by the court and was not allowed to cross-examine witnesses, she did have an attorney present. It was also learned that Catherine had been given a copy of her testimony and had been provided with the ability to make changes. The record also indicated that at the coroner's inquest Catherine was told that she did not have to testify. Landon ruled that her testimony could be read aloud to the jury. Since they were reading from a printed text, Keach would be allowed to make objections before each sentence was read, thus preventing the jury from hearing an objectionable statement. Keach objected to almost every line – generally the judge ruled against him.

In the reading of the testimony, the main point made by the prosecution was the difference between Catherine's account of the incidents and those of her sisters.

The Fan

The extensive media coverage of the trial resulted in numerous reports incorporating little incidents and even rumors. One of the most interesting asides was the tale of the fan. The first day of the trial Catherine had masked her face by wearing a heavy veil. While the two Nolan sisters were in jail they had been befriended by Deputy Curtis, one of the jailors. At the end of the first day's session, Deputy Curtis advised Catherine that the veil might imply that she was trying to hide her guilt. Wisely, Catherine removed the veil for the remainder of the trial. With nothing to protect her face from prying eyes, Catherine took to carrying a fan, which she could open and close as desired. During the trial, *The Troy Times* pointed out that there was a secret to the fan. According to their reports, it was the very same fan that Lizzie Borden carried at her trial (three years before). If the story is true, it is reasonable to assume that the fan was provided by Mrs. McQuirk, the reporter from the *New York World,* who had abandoned objectivity in favor of supporting Catherine and worked for a newspaper that covered both trials.

The kiss

When Charles Winne was called to testify, Catherine's supporters and detractors were treated to a scene straight from a Harlequin novel. As Charles passed Catherine on his way to the witness stand, he bent over and gave her a brief kiss on the cheek. During the Victorian Era, this would be considered a brazen act for a married man to a former lover.

Women on Trial

During the Victorian Era, trials where a woman was the accused usually turned into community spectacles. This sense of exposition was definitely the case with Catherine's trial. The number of people in the audience of the courtroom grew each day the trial lasted. The press was quick to point out that, as the number in attendance grew, so did the percent of those who were female. Even unaccompanied young girls were in the courtroom. It was as if the Catherine Nolan had developed her own groupies.

One of the young women who could not attend the trial was Elizabeth. Following the decision to try the two sisters separately, Elizabeth had been remanded to the county jail. There, from her cell window, she would watch those who came and went from her sister's trial but she could only assume what was happening. Each evening, after Catherine was returned to her cell, the two sisters would review the day's events.

Expert testimony

During the course of the trial, the prosecution placed on the stand four different doctors who testified as to the existence of arsenic in John's body and how the amount found would have caused the death of an individual. These doctors were all experts and, with the possible exception of Dr. Zeh, they had all testified in other trials involving poison. The doctors also told the jury that death from arsenic could occur at any time from within hours of its ingestion up to fifteen days later. They also said that it was not uncommon for a victim who had consumed arsenic to have a period where they would feel better, then have a relapse and die. This was the cycle in John's illness.

Motive is always one of the major issues in a murder trial. It was no different in the case of Catherine Nolan. Three insurance agents were placed on the stand. They told of how they had insured most of the members of the Nolan family (the mother was the one exception). Although the insurance policies were not large, they were equivalent to at least a year's income of the person. The prosecution was hindered because Judge Landon consistently ruled with the defense that any insinuation relating to the deaths of other members of the family were not admissible. His ruling was based on the fact that Catherine faced no charges relating to those deaths and there was not even evidence that the three other family members were murdered.

The prosecution never put forward an argument that the administration of arsenic might be part of an emotional breakdown that Catherine was experiencing. If they had, it would have opened the door to an insanity defense.

There were notable events in the Nolan trial. These included: the defense's discovery of a second Nolan family in Waterford; the testimony of the dying aunt; the persona of one of the key witnesses; the admission of a statement by the family's overused undertaker; a "scientific" experiment; the possible existences of a second source of poison and then, of course, and there was the outcome.

The third day of the trial Keach was able to get into the record that there was a second Nolan family living in Waterford. Like the family of Michael Nolan, the second Nolan family had four daughters, including one named Sarah [the name used in the poison books]. The problem was that the children in the second Nolan family all had very distinguishing red hair, while the Nolans on trial had brown hair. When it looked like the prosecution was going to attack the issue of mistaken identity, Keach backed down. After all, he had raised doubt, even if it was a weak point.

The third day of the trial opened with an assessment of Mrs. Gavin's health by Dr. Balch of Albany. On the first day of testimony, when the prosecution expressed concern about Mrs. Gavin's health, Dr. Balch had been appointed to accompany

Mrs. Gavin on her trip from Stillwater to Ballston Spa. According to the doctor, Mrs. Gavin's health had declined to a point that he feared that if she were required to stand as a witness it might result in heart failure. The doctor's suggestion was the same as the prosecution's, that a statement be taken and entered into evidence. As he had with the reading of Catherine's testimony before the coroner's jury, Keach vehemently objected. Keach was consistent. He opposed the admission of any statement. Keach obviously wanted the impact of any witness to be seen by the jury, not for them to be exposed to just the cold words.

Landon was nothing if not a skeptic. Faced with the possibility that one side was going to lose a key witness, he adjourned the court and personally went to Mrs. Gavin's room to see for himself, her condition. When Landon returned he made a very unusual decision. He instructed the jury; the two sets of attorneys; the court reporter; that he was going to take them to the hotel. He asked the others in the courtroom to remain while he literally took the court to Mrs. Gavin. The *World*'s reporter, Mrs. McQuirk, quickly talked to both sets of lawyers and obtained permission to witness the testimony. Her newspaper account is the only eye witness record known to exist of this unusual session. The emotions and bias shown in this one report from the *World* are significant enough to be carried in full.

"Mrs. Gavin was found propped up with pillows in a room in the hotel, and so obviously nearing her end that all doubt about the statement of her condition vanished at once. Behind her stood her pretty daughter, and beside her was her physician. At her other side was Judge Landon, and rwanged [sic] on the stairway and huddled in the narrow space were the jury, the counsel and court officers. The prisoner was the last in the procession, and, catching site of the aunt's death-like face, threw her arms about her kissed her repeatedly, while the dying woman clutched her [back]. The cousin kissed Catherine, who then sank back into a chair and sat through the brief proceedings.

The clerk of the court administered the oath and the dying woman responded "I will. I will."

Judge Lamoureaux [sic] hurriedly questioned her concerning the care of John Nolan in his last illness. Her answers came convulsively through closed teeth. Counsel for both sides calmed her excitement. She said that John Nolan only drank a teaspoon of the beef tea alleged by the prosecution to have contained arsenic and that she (Mrs. Gavin) drank the balance.

When asked if she gave John any food or drink containing arsenic, the woman said: "I never did," and added excitedly, "Catherine never did poison John."

As the judge was adjourning the court Catherine again darted to her aunt's side and kissed her repeatedly, and then stepped back into a dim corner of the hall, while the jury and Judge filed slowly out.

The old woman as the doctors and attendants removed her into her room and applied restoratives, was still repeating: "Catherine never did it – Catherine never killed John."

"Oh I can't bear [sic] to see my auntie look so!" cried Catherine and then burst into tears, the first she has shed since the trial began.

"But her testimony wasn't against you" said one of those with her.

"I don't care about that; it's poor auntie's condition."

On her way back to the court-house she [Catherine] remarked: "The grass does smell so nice!"

The report is important on two levels. The *World* was not neutral and its bias toward Catherine was obvious in the choice of words. The second is that it provides some indication as to the deep emotions to which the jury was exposed.

News of the adjournment and visit to the hotel had spread through Ballston Spa. As the group was on their way back to the courtroom, the sidewalks were lined by people who had gathered to see the stars of their local drama.

Despite Mrs. McQuirk's account that the prosecution claimed that there was arsenic in the final cup of beef tea; that was never their primary point. The most the prosecution tried to show was that there **may** have been arsenic in Wednesday's beef tea. The case was built on the belief that there ***was*** arsenic in the tea served the previous Friday.

Burt Shaw, the druggist, said that he could not swear that it was Catherine who bought the poison; it might have been Helena. More importantly, Shaw was quick to point out that on

June 29th, Catherine had come to his store and asked him to deny that she ever tried to buy poison because, in her words, "she never had." She went on to tell Shaw that the rumors in the newspapers were annoying her.

It is not what a witness says that matters; it is what the jury hears that counts. What is heard depends heavily on the witness' credibility and demeanor. This persona factor is important with any witness; however, when the person testifying is an "expert" for either side, his or her deportment matters even more. This crossing of content and demeanor was emphasized with Professor Maurice Perkins. Perkins suffered from a common byproduct of being employed in an academic environment; he was a pompous elitist and it showed. Perkins was a true expert regarding the effects of various chemicals on a body and he wanted everyone to know it. Unfortunately for the prosecution he exhibited his enormous ego when he testified in Catherine's trial. In front of a jury of primarily laborers, Keach was able to use Perkins' ego as a lever, pushing impression against fact.

Keach was able to dispel some of the concerns over Elizabeth's not saving the vomit through the testimony of Rose Laversee. Rose was nurse from Cohoes who had stayed with the Nolans for a week when Catherine had been sick the winter previous to John's death. On the stand, Rose said that she had told Elizabeth that when a person was vomiting it was better to bury the waste than to keep it above ground. Laversee's reasoning was that burying the byproduct reduced the likelihood that the disease would spread. Laversee did not tell Elizabeth to ignore Doctor Zeh's orders; her advice given at a very different time and about a different illness.

With the possible exception of Mrs. Gavin, who had actually been a prosecution witness, the most important witness for the defense was Dr. C. Howard Travell of Troy. Travell was thirty years-old and unlike the other "experts," he had only practiced medicine for 18 months. He was also the only physician the defense would put on the stand. Because he was a doctor he was by definition an "expert"; however, his credentials were virtually non existent as compared to the variety of expert witnesses for the prosecution.

With Landon's permission, during a break in the trial a teapot and several cups were brought into the court. When the court reconvened, Travell put on an interesting, if not balanced, chemistry demonstration. In front of the jury, Dr. Travell put grains of arsenic in tea. He did the same "experiment" four times. In each case a residue remained either on the top or on the bottom. He showed that the effect was the same even when the tea was stirred. What he did not explain was that arsenic comes in two forms, one soluble and one that is non-soluble; also that arsenic is almost always a compound containing other elements; these other elements may have been the residue. From experts consulted on this research, it appears Travell used the non-soluble form and put on a "show" for the jury.

Travell had important trait; unlike Perkins, Travell was likable.

Mary, the only sister who took the stand, was called as a witness by both the prosecution and the defense. She was, however, not a strong witness for either side. When asked follow-up questions, she would constantly turn to the clerk and ask, "What did I just say?" During the time the defense had her on the stand she mentioned that there was some "treatment" for bedbugs in the house. Although Mary had no idea the contents of the bedbug treatment, she knew that the remedy was usually kept in an old whiskey bottle in John's room.

Mary also testified that at the time of the lunch on Friday, Catherine was in the family's garden tying up roses. Catherine had said in front of the coroner's jury, in part of the statement read to the trial jury that she was in the sitting room suffering from a headache.

Another example of Mary's inconsistency was in the source of John's illness. At one point in the trial she testified that John had said that it was the mill water that made him sick. Later, Mary said that she never heard John say the cause of his illness.

Interestingly, Keach placed into the record one statement to dispel the money as the motive. The written statement was from Thomas Wall, the Nolan family's frequently used undertaker. Wall's statement was submitted to show that the cost of the funerals had consumed much of the insurance revenues. In addition to the financial statement, Wall had added an interesting comment. It seems that while Helena was at the funeral home selecting her mother's casket, she had indicated that she would be next and had actually picked out her own casket. There is no indication in the records that Helena was suffering from any long-term illness.

The trial ends

The last day of the trial Catherine entered the courtroom carrying a bouquet. Before the session began she was seen greeting some of her associates and well-wishers. This is the first time she had been reported to be social. Her behavior on this day was so out of character with the persona that she had demonstrated in the past, that several accounts said she actually appeared 'animated.'

The prosecution had done all it could. In hindsight it appears that some of the witnesses the prosecution's team had counted on to prove the people's case, Mary and Mrs. Gavin, may have been as much a witness for the defense as for the people. Travell had also been the last of the experts and his visual experiment, although almost definitely staged, may have weighed heavily with the unsophisticated jury.

Both sides closed with relatively short statements. The defense reminded the jury that all it was required to do was to show that the prosecution had not proven beyond a reasonable doubt that Catherine had committed the crime. Of course Keach was playing heavily on Catherine's use of the names "Sarah" and "Sadie" when he told the jury that there "was no proof that Catherine ever had a grain of arsenic in her possession."

At one point Keach went for the emotional jugular stating, "I am defending a girl who apparently has not a friend in the world." The jury had not been in the room when Catherine was being "animated." Keach then had some enjoyment criticizing "expert" witnesses, pointing out the fallibility of their testimony (his own witness, Dr. Travell, included). Keach took a bold step in inferring that Professor Perkins was "fallible"; Perkins was, after all, a nationally recognized expert in his field. His criticism may have been much of a gamble. Keach probably felt that a jury of working men would **not** welcome the testimony of a person paid to be a witness; especially an expert with Perkins's attitude.

It was, however, for Collins that Keach saved his greatest and most caustic attack. Keach pointed out that Collins, as constable, had sought evidence against Catherine; placed himself on the jury and then as he transported her to jail tried to get her to "give information that might incriminate her." So condemning was Keach of Collins' behavior that at one point he compared Collins' treatment to one of the most dictatorial governments in the world at the time saying, "The Czar of Russia was never more vindictive."

The eloquent Judge L'Amoreaux was chosen to deliver the closing statement on behalf of the prosecution. L'Amoreaux comments were direct, concise, and established a logical blueprint for the events in the Nolans' house. L'Amoreaux started the prosecution closing by reminding the jury in dramatic detail of agony that John had experienced. L'Amoreaux noted to the jury that Catherine had sat through the description of her brother's agonizing death without demonstrating any grief.

Throughout his closing remarks L'Amoreaux turned repeatedly toward Catherine and in an accusatory tone asked her rhetorically, "Why did you do this?"

During his closing argument, L'Amoreaux attempted to use Catherine's in court behavior against her. It was not that she appeared sad, angry, fearful, or even relieved that the trial was nearing an end; it was instead her apparent indifference that he wanted to be sure the jury observed. Even when he pointed an accusatory finger directly at her and asked, "Was that poison by the hand of that girl sitting there or did it find its way to John's stomach by accident?" Catherine remained unmoved. She never flinched, her lips did not tighten, nor did tears gather in her eyes. She never once turned her eyes away from his intimidating stare. In point of fact, the newspapers all reported that with the exception of the brief incident with her aunt, Catherine never showed any emotion during the trial. It is hard to envision a person, guilty or not, who faced with a charge of murder, would not exhibit some sensitivity. To those in the audience it was like she was devoid of feelings, almost heartless and that was what L'Amoreaux wanted the members of the jury to remember when they went into their deliberations.

While L'Amoreaux was closing, there was an interesting incident that he turned to his advantage. L'Amoreaux took time to condemn Keach for criticizing Perkins as an expert witness. Keach leaped to his feet and interrupted L'Amoreaux saying, "I have said nothing against Professor Perkins and I wish to say right here that I regard him as an estimable gentleman, who has simply done his duty."

L'Amoreaux was chosen by the prosecution because he was a sage. His performance was the act of a mentor to all the younger attorneys in the room. He responded to Keach's interruption with, "I am glad to hear this confession." Turning yet one more time to Catherine he added, "It is at all times good for the soul."

The prosecution reminded the jury that they should not be swayed by the age or gender of the accused. The prosecution also reminded the jury that they should also not be influenced by Catherine's apparent poverty.

After L'Amoreaux finished his remarks, Judge Landon directed the jury as to what constituted the various degrees of murder. Landon's charge to the jury only took approximately half an hour concluding with the reminder, "The proper way to do its (the jury's) duty was to do it consistently and in absolute determination of purpose to do right." With those words the judge closed the case and sent the jury to deliberate Catherine's fate.

Verdict

Everyone who had been at the trial was amazed when in less than fifteen minutes after the jury was sent to begin its deliberations, there was an announcement that the jury had reached a verdict. Those in attendance were almost in a state of shock. Most had just begun to take a break. Those in the halls had to rush back into the courtroom to learn that, after only one vote, the jury had determined that Catherine was "not guilty." After the jury rendered its verdict, Catherine began to cry. Catherine was taken into the arms of Mrs. McQuirk, the reporter from the *World*, who had long ago given up objectivity in pursuit of a cause. Mrs. McQuirk, who upon hearing the verdict had pushed her way forward, gave Catherine a kiss of congratulations on the cheek.

Through the clamor the defense asked what was to happen with the charges against Elizabeth. District Attorney Pierson said that although they felt they had a solid case, it would not be just to convict a person who they felt played a lesser role after a jury had found the person they felt responsible "not guilty." The judge ordered that all charges be dropped and left the courtroom, only to miss one of the most unusual endings to any trial.

The jury foreman was Isaac Groff, a successful dealer in stones and gravel in Saratoga. After Landon left the room, Groff climbed onto the judge's bench and began banging the gavel. When some semblance of order returned, Groff called out, "As these poor girls have been in jail eight months (it was really nine months) and have not a cent of money, I ask everybody in the court room to contribute to make a purse for them." Immediately, men took off their hats and started passing them among the crowd. In total sixty dollars was raised.

A side note: both Groff and district Attorney Pierson lived just off North Broadway in Saratoga (they were only three houses apart). One can only imagine they way they greeted each other when they met after the trial.

Elizabeth was immediately released and she joined Catherine in their moment of relief. The two sisters took some of their new found money and went to the Medbery Hotel for lunch. After their meal, the sisters returned to the jail picked up their limited personal effects and took the afternoon train to Waterford.

Catherine was interviewed a few days after the trial. She was staying in her attorney, Charles Keach's home. She assured her supporters that she appreciated a real bed. Her intentions were to seek employment and then to provide a home for Mary and Elizabeth. Catherine also remarked that she doubted seriously that she would every return to Waterford.

Post script

The trial ended in April. On June sixth Catherine was again living in Saratoga County. We know that because she filed two claims against the life insurance company for failure to pay in full the claims on her brother's policies. As these two cases developed, Keach was again Catherine's lawyer.

The Nolan Family

In October of 1893 there were eight members of the Nolan family whose names appear in this tale. The parents were Michael and Ellen. The family had moved from Stillwater to Waterford about 8 years before the series of deaths began. Before their move Michael had had a farm near Stillwater. He gave up the farm to work in a local forging plant and Ellen, who was infirmed, did the best she could to maintain the family home. Both parents were born in Ireland and all four of their children were born in the United States. Their oldest daughter was 22 year-old Helena; also called Lena. All three of these members died in a six week period in October and November 1893. The second oldest was 20 year-old Catherine who, for unexplained reasons, was called Sarah and Sadie. The third child, the only son, was 19 year-old John who died in June 1894. The fourth child was 17 year-old Mary. The fifth was 14 year-old Elizabeth also called Eliza, although according to the record, on occasion she also went by the name Lena. The final member was Eliza Gavin, Michael's sister. Eliza Gavin lived in Stillwater; however, when family members became ill, it was her role to nurse them back to health or see them off. The second part of her role had kept her busy for several months.

Elizabeth Bain

"I think he has a knife."

In many ways they were virtually the same as countless other young couples that were out that same night. It was a Sunday evening so there were not many activities for them to enjoy. They were new to each other so they were content just strolling intently into the twilight. Young and in love, the warm July evening was brimming with an allure of romance. It was the kind of gentle evening that called for them to find a place that would be quiet and secluded.

They found themselves walking along the path that connected the hamlet with the mill. Along this path they would come upon a place known locally as the brushy area. There they could sit next to each other under "the big tree," touching in the way that only young lovers can understand. It was after all "their special place." They may not have realized it or even cared but all young couples have that place that is special to them.

They were unnoticed this evening but the people of the village of Schuylerville had seen them walking to this same spot several times before.

The year was 1916 and the couple had often been seen on weekends at the moving pictures. There, in the dark of the theater, they would rub tenderly against each other.

Yes, they were like many other couples out that night, but in one very significant way they were different.

The couple

Her name was Elizabeth Bain, his Robert Parker. At eighteen she was employed as a domestic in the Marshal House the same building that the British had used as a headquarters following the Battle of Saratoga. He worked mixing paints in the wallpaper mill that was a little further up the Hudson River.

At twenty-three he was known for being conscientious and ambitious. Like is father, he worked as a laborer in the local mill but Robert had aspirations. The first was to become an apprentice at the mill in the fall. The supervisors of the mill shared his perceptions of his work habits and had indicated that his objective was reasonable. He was tall and thin. His body was the type you associate with high school boys who have not yet grown the muscle that will eventually fill out their lanky frames.

She, on the other hand, was blessed or cursed by a simple, deep, alluring beauty. Her natural blonde hair made her stand out in any crowd. Her heart-shaped face was the type that caught and held men's attention. Her womanly shape was usually hidden under the loosely draped clothing of the period, but men still noticed her narrow waist.

She had been born to abject poverty. Had she been born to a professional family she would have made an excellent debutant. But then, had she been born in a middle class family, there may never have been a story to tell.

The fateful night

As was their custom, the couple had met at her residence at 7:00 p.m. On this July evening, like so many before, they sat on the stoop for a while talking about their dreams and desires. It was the type of conversation shared by other couples their age. As it grew darker she suggested they take a walk and enjoy the night air. They both knew that a walk would take them out of the meddling eye of her employer.

When he left his home to meet her he had taken along a bottle of beer for them to share. After walking to her residence from his family's apartment in Schuylerville, the beer had gotten warm and unappealing. As they walked along the path he drank half the contents of the bottle. Elizabeth, perhaps because she knew the effects alcohol had had on her family, refused even a swallow. As they walked along he poured the remainder of the contents of the bottle onto the ground.

Parker saw himself as a gentleman and didn't want his companion to get her dress stained on the grass or dirty from the worn patches of bare earth along the trail. Ever the gentleman, he had found an old box for her to sit on. In the warm darkness of this July evening the couple sat under their special tree. The place they chose to rest was near a pair of gates that led to a barn used by a local farmer to store hay. They assumed they were alone to share the imaginings of a future together.

Suddenly, they heard rustling in the bushes around them. Looking up, Elizabeth thought she recognized the man that came out of the bushes. Parker also thought he recognized him and said, "Did you follow us?" Although the man answered "no," the couple believed that he had in fact pursued them to their nest. The man, who was twice their age, began to talking pointlessly about some bicycle. The more he talked the more excited he became.

Elizabeth knew the man and said to Parker, "Let's go home." No sooner had she muttered the words when she called out to Rob, "He has something in his hand. Maybe it's a knife!" The man's hand was clutching something in his jacket pocket.

The couple hustled to leave. Meanwhile, the intruder started to move in their direction cutting off their retreat. Feeling threatened, Parker asked, "What do you have in your hand?"

"Damn you, I'll show you what I've got," the man answered as he reached even deeper into his pocket.

At a time like this there are only two ways to react. One either has to flee or attack. Parker, perhaps because he was being the protector or possibly because he realized that the long skirts that were in fashion at the time would have hindered Elizabeth's ability for flight, chose to grab the arm of the interloper. The two men began to wrestle in what was a mismatch. The intruder was older and stronger than Parker. Elizabeth tried to help her lover by grabbing the man from behind. The man was brawny with more muscle power than the couple's combined strength. As she tried to help her lover, the man literally brushed Elizabeth aside with one arm. The force of his swing sent Elizabeth against a tree. Her head struck with such force that a swelling occurred. Freed from their grasp, the man then took his attack to the next level saying repeatedly to Parker, "I'll kill you." The man repeated the threat several times, while resuming his attack on Parker. Realizing that he was out-muscled and in desperation, Parker called out to Elizabeth, "Hit him with something!"

Elizabeth grabbed the empty beer bottle and began to hit the man on the head. After the second blow the man went down, pulling Parker with him. On the ground, the man dug at Parker's eyes with his fingernails. Elizabeth continued hitting at the man's head with the heavy glass bottle until it broke. Whether from the effects of the blows to the head or in an effort to get a better hold at a different place, the man yielded some of his grip on Parker. Parker was not free enough to flee but he was able to regain his footing. The man continued to hold onto one of Parker's legs. To free himself Parker kicked the man, who had not gotten up. The man reacted by grabbing Parker's pant leg holding on to the material so that Parker could not get in a full swing. It was the wrong move. Adrenaline flowing, Parker continued to kick the man in the head with his free leg. The kicking continued until the man was still. Parker would later say that he only meant to kick until the man released his pants.

Filled with fear and desperation, the couple fled the scene. When they reached the welcoming glare of a street light, Elizabeth could see blood on Parker's face and coat. There was even blood on her sweater. The compassionate lover, Elizabeth inquired about Parker's injuries. It was soon established that Parker's injuries were minor. The blood had to be from the other man. With so much blood on Parker they realized that the other man must be seriously injured. Full of dread and trepidation they went back to check on the man's condition.

When they got back to the big tree they could see that the man was completely still. Although neither were doctors, when they saw that the prone man had not moved at all, they presumed he was dead. Looking around they could see that there was a great deal of blood on the ground from the beating. Consumed by fear, Elizabeth said in the local dialect, "We will be arrested sure."

The couple talked for a few minutes trying to determine the best course of action. Like so many others who react out of panic, they decided that it would be best to hide the body rather than admit what happened. They grabbed the man by the legs and pulled his body through a small field and up to a barn full of hay. Elizabeth did not go inside the dark building but left the final purging to Parker. While Parker dragged the body inside, Elizabeth started for her home. Parker stuck the body face down in the dry hay. Then he rushed out of the barn to catch up with Elizabeth.

Scared and full of anxiety, the couple walked back to the Marshal Place where Elizabeth had her room. Parker came inside and used a wash basin to clean the blood off himself as best he could. His head was cooling down from the panic of the fight and the realization that he had probably killed another man. When he finished washing he decided that he should leave. He told Elizabeth that on his way back to his own house he would stop at the barn and cover the body with hay. Hopefully, he could conceal it enough that it would provide them with more time to think before the body was discovered.

After Parker left her room, Elizabeth washed the blood off her sweater and person as best she could. She found that the blood had stained the sweater and would not come out of the material. Probably as a result of her poverty, Elizabeth did not throw the sweater away. Instead, she folded the stained garment and placed it back in her dresser.

Parker gone, Elizabeth sat alone wondering the fate that would curse her now.

Parker was a man of action. As he had promised Elizabeth, he went from her room back to the barn. Even in the limited glow of the moon, the man's body was obvious. Parker tried to cover the corpse with loose hay. When he returned to the doorway, Parker turned back toward the center of the room to survey his work. He realized that the body, even covered by the hay, would be easily spotted by anyone who entered. Alone, and without the counsel of Elizabeth, Parker elected to set fire to the barn. He hoped that the intensity of the heat would consume the body or, at the very least, destroy any evidence that the man had died from an assault. As has been the case in numerous other situations in history, Parker used fire in an attempt to cover a greater crime. As the flames began to consume the building, Parker slipped out into a field where he laid in the cover of the tall grass.

The barn was filled with tons of dry hay. This was before hay was tightly bailed. Stored loose hay makes an excellent fuel. Soon the heat of the blaze was intense. The locals, all of whom came out to see the fire, soon gave up on saving the barn and focused their efforts on ensuring that the blaze would not spread.

Elizabeth was among those who came out to watch the fire.

After a substantial crowd had gathered at the fire, Parker rose from the grass and slipped silently back into the village of Schuylerville. In his family's apartment he tried desperately, but to no avail, to wash the blood from his clothes. Eventually, he gave up and put on clean clothes. Alone he went down to the bridge that crossed the Hudson and threw the clothes he had worn that evening into the swift water. As the clothes moved down stream with the current, Parker had to hope his life would likewise be able to move on.

But different

Yes, they were like so many other young couples. There was, however, one major difference between Robert Parker and Elizabeth Bain and most other couples out that night. At eighteen, **Elizabeth had been married for almost three years.** The man that they had beaten until he was dead was her estranged husband. Before taking too firm a stand as to the values of anyone involved in this tale, understand that this is not a happy story for anyone. Then again, the tale is not as direct as some would try to have it painted.

Elizabeth Stover

Elizabeth Bain had been born across the Hudson River in Washington County. Her humble home was in the shadow of Bald Mountain (a true irony – even the mountain was not all that was expected, being in fact only a hill).

Her maiden name had been Stover and her childhood had been spent in hopeless poverty. The best that could be said for her father was that he worked occasionally. To earn money to support the family, her mother, who was unskilled, was required to work as a laborer in farmers' fields and cutting wood. So desperate for money was her mother that she took jobs where she worked alongside men, not women. Her father was also usually alongside men, the difference was he was on a stool at the local tavern.

When Elizabeth was young the industrial revolution was in full swing. America needed an educated workforce. To create that employable base, the common schools were becoming a required part of every child's life. Without the benefit of parents who believed in the promise of an education, if it had not been of the insistence of the truant officer who had to visit the Stover house frequently, Elizabeth would probably never have acquired her limited ability to read and write.

At nine, Elizabeth began working in the fields beside her mother. Barely able to lift anything substantial, she was still required to help earn money to help the family. By fifteen her quality of life was improving. She had been given a position as a domestic in the home of a farmer in nearby South Argyle. As a domestic, she had room and board and a real house to live in, not the shanty she had inhabited all her life.

It was at South Argyle that thirty-five year old, Peter Ransom Bain, noticed Elizabeth in the yard of the farm house. Bain was working nearby as a farmhand. Bain went by both Peter and Ransom. Despite the twenty year age difference, Bain came around one afternoon telling Elizabeth that her brother had sent him. Before he left, Bain asked if he might call again that night. His visits didn't stop there. He visited three evenings a week for almost a month. Although he had only known Elizabeth for a brief period, he asked her to marry him. In the custom of the day, or perhaps in an effort to not answer, she told Peter that he had to ask permission of her mother. By this time Elizabeth's natural father was dead and her mother had remarried into the Durling family (small world this was, the same family that appears in the book *Maggie's Revenge*).

As instructed by Elizabeth, Bain went to visit Cora Durling to ask her permission to have her daughter's hand in marriage. Bain assured Cora that he would be a "good provider." Bain guaranteed Cora, a woman who had spent her life struggling to meet the needs of her family, that Elizabeth would not want for the necessities of life. Today, many of us buy lottery tickets in hopes that our dreams will be satisfied. Life had kicked Cora so often and so hard that she had simpler aspirations. Believing what her daughter's suitor said about himself, Cora thought her daughter had hit the jackpot with Peter Bain's offer of marriage.

Later, when Cora visited her daughter to talk about the wedding, Elizabeth told her mother that she didn't love Bain. Cora pressed her daughter to marry him anyway. In November 1913, just after her 16th birthday, Elizabeth Stover stood before the Rev. Dr. Webster of South Argyle and became Mrs. Bain.

Mrs. Elizabeth Bain

From the beginning the marriage proved it was not all that was promised. On the day after their wedding the couple attended a dance. It was one of Elizabeth's first social events. Peter, who never actually danced, used the occasion to socialize. While others were on the dance floor, he went off to visit with some of the men. Seeing the beautiful blonde sitting alone, a young man in attendance boldly asked Elizabeth to join him on the dance floor. When Peter came back into the room, he found his wife with the young stranger dancing on the crowded floor. Peter swaggered onto the dance floor, grabbed his wife and pulled her into another room. There he scolded her loudly telling her that she should never dance with another man. Timid and embarrassed, the child bride left the room and the party.

Everyone, other than Elizabeth's mother, felt Peter was lacking in ambition and worth. Even those who expected little soon learned that Peter was less than they expected.

After the incident at the dance, the couple went south to Schaghticoke where they spent some time with Elizabeth's sister and her husband. After the wedding, it turned out that Peter was unemployed (something neither Elizabeth nor her mother knew). Without an income, the couple was forced to spend the following winter with two of his brothers and one of their wives in a small community between Greenwich and Argyle called Rock Hill.

It was not until March of 1914 that Peter finally took a job working as a laborer on the Todd farm in South Argyle. Now he was earning living of $26 a month. As was often the case with farm work, as part of the employment package the couple was able to reside in the tenant house for free. Since they needed a strong laborer, Peter was able to take his meals with the Todd family. Since she wasn't working for the family, when it came to food Elizabeth had to fend for herself. Without the support of his family, Peter was suddenly did not provide for Elizabeth the way he had said he would. During the period that they lived at the Todd farm, there was often little or no food in the Bain's house. Things were so bad that Elizabeth would walk from Dutchtown to her mother's home at Bald Mountain to get a decent meal.

In exasperation over her marriage, hunger and life in general, Elizabeth looked for a job of her own. As summer came she was finally able to obtain a position as a domestic at the hotel on Cossayuna Lake.

Elizabeth had to walk 2 1/2 miles to work each morning. The walk in the dark would have consumed the better part of an hour. The problem was compounded by the hotel's expectation that she be at work at 5:30 each morning. To be on time she had to get up at 4:00 a.m. Elizabeth maintained the schedule for a while, but finally asked her employer if she might have a room, rather than travel each day. In the old hotels, like rural resorts of today, the help was provided with rooms in buildings on the property but not in the main lodge. Understanding her situation, the owner consented to Elizabeth's request for housing. Elizabeth moved from one set of poor surroundings at the tenant house to another just slightly better in the dorms at the hotel.

Bain shows up

It was the second night that Elizabeth stayed at the hotel that Bain showed up. He stormed into the hotel's kitchen where he made a scene, beseeching his wife to come home with him to the tenant house. At the time of his unexpected visit, Elizabeth was still working her shift. Even though she was supposed to be working, Bain would not leave her alone. Eventually, he caused such a commotion that the hotel's owner ordered him out of the building. Bain left the building but not the property, choosing instead to wait outside the kitchen for his wife. Eventually, her shift ended and she headed for her room in the outbuilding to change her clothes.

As Elizabeth tried to walk across the yard to her room, Bain clung to her. In her room he again prevailed upon her to return to the farm. She refused saying that she wanted to live at the hotel where she could have some life. A life to this married adolescent meant spending the evening watching the hotel's guests dance. Bain's jealous nature could not stand even this amount of socializing by his wife. The argument continued until, in anger and out of frustration, Elizabeth told her husband that she did not want to live with him any longer. Angry and dejected, Bain went back to the tenant's house and Elizabeth went to watch the hotel's guests dance.

To some, Bain's behavior was a demonstration of love. To others it was a most pure demonstration of domination. In most ways he treated his child bride less like a partner and more like a possession. In the circles that he traveled in, husbands and wives were rarely passionate or even affectionate so it was easy for him to confuse the feelings he harbored for Elizabeth.

The dance is over

The hotel on the lake was only open for the season. When it closed at the end of the summer of 1914, Elizabeth faced a choice. She elected not to return to the tenant's house, but instead went to move back to her mother's humble house.

Bain, who was a contemporary of Elizabeth's mother, was able to make more persuasive arguments to Cora than to his own wife. After Elizabeth had lived with her mother for three weeks, Ransom Bain visited the house. With the support of Cora, Bain was able to manipulate Elizabeth into returning to him.

The harvest season over, Bain was again unemployed. The couple returned to his brother, Wesley's home in South Argyle. This was the same residence they had lived in the previous winter. The earnings that Bain had made on the Todd farm were all gone, so they decided to make some money by holding a dance at his brother's home. It was at dances, amidst the social companionship of people of all ages, that the troubles between the Bains consistently transitioned from simmering to boiling and then to overflowing.

At this dance Bain's distrust for his wife was evident. In an effort to be able to do his duties as host and to keep track of Elizabeth, Bain told Cora to keep an eye on her daughter. That night, after the dance, the couple had another fight. Elizabeth had had enough of his accusations and left her husband for a second time. With no other place to go, Elizabeth again returned to her mother's home.

In March of 1915, Bain hit the employment jackpot when he obtained employment at Funston's lumber yard in Schuylerville. With his new found earnings, he rented an apartment and again prevailed upon Cora Durling to intercede and send Elizabeth back to him. This time, as each time in the past, Bain promised that now he could and would provide for her daughter. Anxious to have one less mouth to feed, Cora took Bain's side and told her daughter that she should return to her husband. In late March 1915, the Bains had again taken up residence together. Despite his promises to take better care of Elizabeth, Bain still provided little for her to eat. On one occasion her mother visited and asked for a cup of tea. Cora was surprised that her daughter was so "neglected" that she did not even have a simple supply of tea in the home. Exactly how Bain was spending his limited income is not clear. It is known that they were forced to move by their landlord for failure to pay the rent. It also known that Bain was arrested at least once in Fort Edward for public intoxication.

The Parkers and the Bains

The house the Bains first moved into in Schuylerville was called an apartment block. One of the other apartments was occupied by the Parker family which was made up of "old man Parker" (Henry); his daughter, Miss Ethel; and Robert, who went by the name Rob. There was another sister who was already married and living with her husband when the Bains moved into the building. The Parkers were a tight knit family who worked hard and, although humble, tried to be upstanding citizens. The family was of the struggling labor class but had not experienced anything near the poverty that had existed in both Bain and Elizabeth's lives.

Perhaps because of the couple's history or more likely because she could not abide her husband, when Elizabeth first moved to Schuylerville she was unhappy and stayed almost exclusively in their small apartment. Although there is no statement either way, there is also the possibility that Elizabeth kept to herself to avoid the wrath of her husband when he was jealous. This was, after all, the first time the couple had ever lived in a community that was actually the size of a village and Bain would have many more people to be jealous of.

In all probability it because of young and virtuous Ethel Parker that, in early May, Bain introduced himself and his wife to the Parkers. In private conversations, he prevailed upon the Parkers to help him make his wife cheerful. Obviously Bain could tell that Elizabeth was not happy. He feared that if things did not change Elizabeth would leave him again. Bain went so far as to ask the Parkers to reinforce his belief that she should remain with her husband at all costs.

Old man Parker may not have been sophisticated but he was wise. From only short meetings he could sense that there was something seriously amiss with the Bains. He could also see that the natural attractiveness of Elizabeth could be a strong temptation for his son. He warned Rob to stay away from their neighbor and stressed that it included keeping away from his neighbor's wife. At this point it is unclear if Robert, the dutiful son, did as his father requested.

Rob's feelings for Elizabeth at the time they lived in the same apartment building are not known but it is understood that he had never "kept company" with any other young woman. (Keeping company is roughly the equivalent of going steady.) On at least one occasion Ransom had invited Robert to meet with Elizabeth and himself at one of the local hotels (ostensibly the purpose of the meeting would have been to share a beverage).

The owner of one of the hotels in Schuylerville would say that he had seen Rob and Elizabeth together, without Bain, in the parlor of his establishment a year before the murder. This would have been in the timeframe that the two families lived in the same apartment building. This hotel owner was the only person who put the couple together this early. In the true sentiment of temperance that was sweeping the country (the Constitutional Amendment that would make alcohol illegal was only three years away), the one newspaper that carried this report of a possible immoral link also pointed out that the hotel in question served alcoholic drinks. There is no statement that the two did in fact have any beverage while they were at the hotel or that they were intimate at the time.

Bain's belief that the Parkers could help make Elizabeth want to stay with him proved unsuccessful. In September of 1915, after a reconciliation of seven months, Elizabeth Bain left her husband for the third time. As was her practice, she moved back in with her mother. This time, before she left, Elizabeth had made it clear that she would never return to her husband.

It took her only a week to find employment as a domestic in the hamlet of Fort Miller. The position included room and board. Four months later, January 1916, she was unemployed. Elizabeth again returned to her mother's house where Bain again tried to have her return. At this time Elizabeth wrote to her husband telling him she would never return to his home. In words that would later be used against her, she said that she was too much of a "sport" for him. In March of 1916, Elizabeth was able to gain employment as a domestic in a residence just north of Schuylerville. From that date until the night under the big tree, Elizabeth was in the employ of Mrs. Walker.

The Walkers lived in what is known as the Marshal House. Along with her meager salary, Elizabeth was given room and board. It was after Elizabeth took this position that she and Rob Parker began to see each other regularly. The mill where Parker was employed was near the house where Elizabeth worked. He had to pass her home each day as he walked to and from work.

As their relationship developed, Rob came to see her at least once a week and often as frequently as three times a week. Unlike Bain's visits three years earlier, Elizabeth enjoyed having young Parker drop by.

The deed is discovered

The day after the barn burned, a local farmer named William G. Ruff went out to gather his dairy cows for the morning milking. In the summer it was his practice to milk the cows outside rather than take them into a hot barn. This choice also meant he did not have to waste time cleaning the barn after the cows were put out for the day. To avoid the direct sun, Ruff would gather the cows under the shade of a big tree. On this morning, as he gathered his herd, he noticed several pools of what looked like blood in a small ravine. Looking closer, Ruff could see bent and broken grass; the signs indicated that something or someone had been pulled up the ravine. The rough trail of bent grass and blood stains led across a small field. He followed the bloody trail for about 150 feet to the side of the burnt out shell of the Chubb barn. As he looked into the charred remains of the barn, he thought he saw what may have been a person's corpse.

As Ruff looked up from the form, he noticed that there were a group of boys poking in the burnt rubble on the other side of what had been the barn. Ruff called the boys over and pointed out what he saw. He told the boys to maintain a close vigil while he went for help. Boys being boys and with the prospect of having the biggest news of the summer in front of them, a couple of boys stayed to watch the scene and the rest left to switch on the rumor machinery. Could there be many more important stories in a boy's lifetime than the one where he found a corpse, better yet, if the person had been murdered?

News of a tragedy spreads quickly in a small town. By the time Ruff found a phone and came back to the remains of the barn, a small group of people had already congregated around the rubble. Those present waited patiently for the police. As they waited there was much speculation, focusing mostly on the corpse being that of a woman.

When the local authorities got to the scene they determined that Ruff was correct when he had told them that he felt that he had found the torso and head of a person. The arms and legs had been so severely burned that they had been cremated by the intense heat of the fire. The missing arms and legs were reported in several newspapers as an indication that the victim had been butchered. In fact, the heat of the fire the night before had caused the limbs to incinerate. The fire had burned up and the underside of the body, which had been face down on the cool earth, was virtually untouched by the heat.

The local officers didn't touch the remains until District Attorney McKelvey arrived at the scene. Despite the rumor that the body of a woman had been discovered, when McKelvey, with the help of an undertaker, turned the body over, it was discovered that the remains were those of a man. More important to their investigation was the fact that clothes the victim was wearing were virtually intact.

Examining the clothing, they found a pocket watch with a chain. On the chain was a fob (a small metal attachment used for identification or decoration), a popular attachment at the time. The initials on the fob were P. R. B. The local police felt that the body probably belonged to Peter Ransom Bain. In addition to the watch and fob, they were also able to find a tobacco box, peg teeth, a tie, a wallet with change and a pocket knife. These items were all quickly traced to Ransom Bain.

Peter Ransom Bain

Peter Bain was from a large family that had settled in the area of Argyle, in Washington County. His life had been spent as a laborer working as a farmer, in day jobs and when lucky, landing a position that lasted a full season. He considered himself a lucky man when he was able to get a job as a laborer in Funston's lumber yard. Bain initially took the job in the lumber yard in 1915, the year before his death. This was when he had prevailed upon Cora Durling to send her daughter to live with him in Schuylerville. In the early spring of 1916, Bain lost his position at Funston's lumberyard. Without any income he could not pay his rent, so he moved back to Bald Mountain (just across the Hudson from Schuylerville) to live. For a while he held a series of short term or day labor positions during the spring, including one where he worked on the roads in the town of Greenwich.

Even though he was not residing or working in Schuylerville, Bain made a practice of visiting the village frequently. While visiting Schuylerville, Bain learned that his wife was often seen with Parker. On several of his visits he told some of the men he knew from working at the lumber yard that he would get Parker. So certain were these men that Bain was sincere in his threat that they told Parker to watch out that Bain was "laying" for him. The threats were considered very real as they went so far as to say Bain had a shotgun. To the misfortune of everyone involved, in the late spring, Bain got a job as a night watchman at the Funston Coal Yard in Schuylerville.

Elizabeth's position in the Marshal House just north of the

village put her within reach of Bain. The local police would say that before the fire, they were aware that there were problems between the couple and between Bain and Parker. As was found common in marriages where one party clearly dominates the other, there was a mixed perception of how Bain felt about his wife. Some people reported that he was deeply in love with his Elizabeth. Others might argue with equal vigor that he wanted to possess her. Whether it was love or possession, Bain constantly wanted Elizabeth with him. The officers who investigated Ransom's death soon learned that he had demonstrated that he did not want her with any other man, especially Parker.

In the spring of 1916, Parker, Bain and Elizabeth all lived within a few miles of each other. It soon became apparent that a clash between the lovers and the spouse was inevitable. Parker was so concerned that in March he ordered a pistol from a catalog. Although he failed to get the necessary permit, it was well known around Schuylerville that on occasion he had carried the gun in public. The gun in question was a small .22 caliber pistol. This is among the smallest caliber handguns.

In contrast to Parker, in May, Bain put in for a permit to carry a pistol. The town justice, who was in charge of issuing permits, denied Bain's request saying there was no need for him to carry a concealed weapon. It was later established that the justice believed that Bain intended to threaten his wife with the pistol and for that reason the permit was denied. Bain appealed claiming he needed the gun for his work as a night watchman. The justice offered a compromise offering to give Bain a pistol permit with the restriction that it was only valid when he was a work. Further, Bain would have to leave the gun in the hands of Mr. Funston when he was not at work. Bain refused to accept the limits. Instead of the desired pistol, Bain purchased a shotgun for which no permit was required.

Realizing an issue was developing, the justice who denied Bain's request reported to Parker that Bain wanted to carry a handgun. At that point Parker was on notice that his safety was in jeopardy.

Now that he was again working in Schuylerville, Bain was proving to be a nuisance for Elizabeth. On at least one occasion he had hidden in the brush outside her window at the Marshal house. Although at the time there was no such charge as stalking, Bain's behavior would have probably met today's definition. Mrs. Walker, Elizabeth's employer, warned Bain that if he were found hanging around in the bushes again she would have him arrested. The charge would have had to have been trespassing.

Bain had a reason for watching Elizabeth, who was still legally his wife. Elizabeth's employer acknowledged that on occasion she had entertained Parker alone in her room in the house. The implication of what occurred when a married woman, or any woman, entertained a man alone in her sleeping chamber was clear to those of this era. At this time, Mrs. Walker's simple comment would suffice as to what occurred in the room; there would not be a need for any further explanation.

Investigation

With the fob containing initials, and knowing the situation between Parker, Elizabeth and Bain, Chief O'Brien of the Schuylerville Police went to the Marshal House to talk to Elizabeth. Alone and without council present, the chief told her of her husband's death and implied strongly that it was a murder. O'Brien bluffed telling Elizabeth that he had found her fingerprints and locks of her hair at the scene of the crime (neither statement was true). Elizabeth immediately broke down and told the story as she remembered it. To her detriment she said she "had helped kill Ransom." This statement, which included the comment that the young couple was surprised by Bain, was repeated later in front of a scribe. There are several key points about her statement. First, although the country did not have Miranda rights, New York State had provisions in the laws that were very similar. In 1916, all suspects were entitled to an attorney during *questioning*. At the trial, the scribe would claim he did not ask *questions* of Elizabeth but only recorded what she had volunteered. This would prove questionable to everyone who heard or read the statement. Included in Elizabeth's explanation was an admission that she had an intimate physical relationship with Parker. At this time, because she was married, such a relationship was illegal.

While Elizabeth was giving her statement to the scribe, the officers went to the mill where Parker was employed. Schuylerville being a small town, Rob knew the officers. Foolishly he opened with the statement, "Too bad about Bain getting burned in that fire." Since until that time the rumor was that a woman had been found, the police were sure they had the perpetrator. While they were at the mill they asked Parker what he knew of the incident. After listening for a few minutes they took Parker to the local station where he, like Elizabeth, confessed. Both had done so without the benefit of counsel. There was one key statement Parker put in his initial statement that was later retracted. In the first interview and before he had council present, Parker said that he had thrown Bain's knife into the fire. The importance to Parker was that the presence of a knife would have made his actions, up to the moving of the body and the lighting of the fire, self-defense. The lack of a weapon and the fire implied that he felt he had something to hide. Apparently Parker did not realize that Bain really did have a knife with him that night.

The district attorney felt he had enough of a case and ordered that Elizabeth and Parker be taken to the jail in Ballston Spa.

Be careful what you write

When the body was positively identified, a couple of officers were assigned to contact members of Bain's family. The officers asked for permission to search Bain's humble residence. Among his belongings they found several letters. One of the letters in the collection was written by Elizabeth to Bain the previous winter. In the letter she said that she hated Bain and that she would never live with him again. This was the letter where she described herself as a "sport."

Included in the collection was one letter that was addressed to Bain but not signed. The unsigned letter requested Bain to meet the writer in front of the Marshal House the following Thursday. Of equal importance was a request that Bain bring the letter with him to the meeting. The person who wrote the letter closed with "You know who this is." To District Attorney McKelvey, the discovery of the letters meant that the final "i" had been dotted and all the "t's" had been crossed. To him it was obvious Bain had been induced to come to the Marshal house so that the lovers could kill him. In McKelvey's mind the couple wanted Bain to bring the letter so that they could then take it from him and destroy it so it would not be incriminating evidence.

Among the other items found was an un-mailed letter to Elizabeth from Bain. In this letter Bain implored yet again that she return to him. Although the letter had never been mailed so Elizabeth would not know of its contents, to the district attorney the note showed that Bain loved his wife and wanted her back. This letter had a troubling sketch. At the bottom where a signature would normally be placed was the drawing of two revolvers. This sketch was done by Bain, not Parker.

In talking with Bain's neighbors in Washington County, two other significant facts came out. These both took away from the seemingly straight forward conclusion drawn from the letters. First, Bain told one of his neighbors that he had gone to the Marshal house on Saturday night. This was the night before the fight and fire. Bain had said that "no one was about" so he planned to go back the next night. Since no assault had taken place, the importance of the unsigned letter as a lure was to some degree nullified. Obviously, Bain was not living in fear. Of equal importance was Bain's attempt to sell his woodstove (not something that there is a huge market for in July). He told one potential buyer that he had "one thing to do," then he was leaving the area so he would not need the stove for the next winter, but did need the money at this time.

The investigation included interviews of several people in Schuylerville who knew the parties. These dialogs led to some other interesting stories. It was learned that Bain occasionally rode his bicycle to the village. Biking as a pastime was in its prime. Having a bicycle gave Bain something, besides Elizabeth, that others coveted. On one occasion he was letting others take a ride on his bike as he talked to his old neighbors. One of the men he talked to was the former police chief of Fort Edward. The ex-chief asked if Bain was concerned about Parker. Adding salt to the wound, the ex-chief reminded Bain that Parker was well liked, continuing with a statement to the effect that if anything were to happen, Parker's friends would take his side. Bain said that he wasn't worried and patted his jacket pocket saying, "I have a little help with me."

Bain was not the only one who was supposedly carrying a weapon. One night a couple of weeks before the fire, Parker was playing pool at one of the taverns in the village. As he was getting ready to leave, a couple of his fellow patrons started to give him some of that ribald humor that men, left in clusters, exhibit toward one of their own if he becomes a new lover. The men were teasing Parker unmercifully about having a "girl." The razing evolved into comments being made about her husband and any threats that may have been issued. Parker assured them he had the situation in hand when he said, "If her fellow bothers me…" at which point he drew his mail order revolver from one of his pockets.

Two days after the fire and the day after their initial confessions, Elizabeth Bain and Robert Parker were brought back to Schuylerville for arraignment. By this time newspapers could print pictures. In would resemble the police being televised escorting a preparatory today the officers who arrested the couple posed with Elizabeth and Parker standing between them.

The two lovers were charged with murder in the first degree and denied bail. Hearing the charge, Elizabeth broke down and sobbed before the judge. Parker remained strong. Before they were taken back to Ballston Spa to await trial, the pair were examined by a doctor who said they showed no signs of injury from a fight. This diagnosis was a problem since at the trial Parker was able to show marks on his shins that were attributed to the fight months before.

The Trial

A local trial of this magnitude, especially because it involved tragedy, emotion, immoral conduct, combined with founded and unfounded rumors, would have been expected to dominate the local media. At almost any other time in Saratoga County's history this would have been the case. Unfortunately for the record, the trial was the last week of October and first week of November 1916. A locally born politician was running for President on the Republican ticket. Charles Evans Hughes, of Glens Falls, had served as Governor of New York and was expected, at least locally, to beat the incumbent Woodrow Wilson. Wilson had been narrowly elected in 1912 only because former President Teddy Roosevelt had split the Republic party when he created the Bull Moose Party. With the Republicans united and Europe at War, it was expected that Hughes would win the election the next week. The news of Hughes' campaign would dominate the local newspapers at the time of the trial. Charles Evans Hughes lost the election two days after the verdict was announced. *Governor Charles Evans Hughes was of no known relation to lawyer Charles Hughes of Washington County who represented several persons in other stories in this series.*

The trial of Elizabeth Stover Bain and Robert Parker was one of the foremost social events of the fall season in Ballston Spa (the county seat). The first day the courtroom was filled with the men who had been called to possibly serve on the jury. Their seats were taken in subsequent days by spectators who comprised the curious, callous, caring, condemning and just plain inquisitive. Like those among us who watch television today just so we can see who is arrested, these people wanted to see for themselves the couple about whom so much had been rumored and written.

Two hundred men had received calls for jury duty. It took a day and a half and fifty-eight men to find twelve suitable jurors. Of the twelve that were selected, eleven were farmers. The remaining juror was a carpenter. The number one reason for perspective jurors to be excused was to say that they had a moral objection to the death penalty. The charge of murder in the first degree was punishable by the electric chair.

There are numerous charges that can be filed in a case involving a wrongful death. District attorneys can ask for anything from premeditated murder to manslaughter. In a decision that did not surprise anyone in the area, District Attorney Lawrence McKelvey went into court seeking a conviction on the most serious offense, Murder in the first degree.

For the charge of Murder in the first degree, which carried the death penalty, to hold up in court, the prosecution would need to show premeditation on the part of the accused. McKelvey would have to convince the jury that the note found in Bain's home, asking that he meet some unnamed person in front of the Marshal House, was meant to lure him to his death. He would be hindered by the fact that the note in question was dated June 27, almost a month before the assault. The note read:

I am going away soon and want to see you before I go. Will you meet me in the road in front of the Marshall place on Thursday night and perhaps there will be someone else there you want to see. We can talk over old times and the future. If you can be there at fifteen minutes before nine o'clock. Please don't tell anyone who wrote the letter and bring it with you because I want to see it tore up. You probably know who this is.

The defense would argue that the note was intended to provide an opportunity for Elizabeth Bain to try to convince her husband to give her a divorce so that she might marry Parker. It is probable that the defense did not play hard enough the fact that there was almost a month between the letter and the assault, or that the letter asked for a meeting on a Thursday and incident was on a Sunday.

The defense was led by attorney Henry Toohey of Schuylerville. Toohey, who was only 31 years-old at the time of the trial, was faced with his first and only capital trial. The facts of the case were not in dispute and little new information emerged at the trial. To a large part the pertinent information had already been carried in the local newspapers in the days following the fire. The issues in question were the character of those involved and the jurors' perception of those individuals. During the trial Parker was quiet and appeared unmoved by the events transpiring in front of him. In contrast, Elizabeth took an active role. She was often seen whispering and consulting with her attorney.

The principle legal issue was premeditation, to which the unsigned letter was important. Toohey acknowledged in court that the unsigned note was written by Parker.

The prosecution could not be sure if either member of the couple were going to testify and if so, what he or she would say. To show that any statements the couple might make could not be trusted, the prosecution wanted to get the statements given by the two young lovers the day Bain's body was found, admitted into the record. In addition to these statements functioning as confessions, there were two very key elements in the statements that the prosecution wanted included. The first was that Elizabeth acknowledged that when her husband had tried to get up she had laid on him to hold him down. This was while Parker kicked him into unconsciousness.

The second reason for wanting the statements in record was that in his first statement, Parker said he threw a knife that had belonged to Bain into the barn – this would have implied self defense. In a follow up statement Parker said there was no knife. There were two implications in Parker's two statements. The first was that he had lied in the first statement so the jury should look at him as a person who did not tell the truth. Additionally, without Parker knowing about a knife there was no need for the couple to claim self defense. Further, if one accepted that there was not a feeling of intimidation on the part of Parker, a beating of this magnitude was unnecessary.

After strong arguments against admissibility, Supreme Court Judge Edward Whitmyer ruled that the statements made by the lovers could be entered as evidence. It is doubtful if these same statements, taken in the same way, would have been admitted today. This is one case where the evolution of the trial system and not the evolution of forensic evidence may have changed the outcome.

Prosecution

District Attorney McKelvey presented the case as two lovers who wanted to be together. He held that despite Elizabeth's desire for a divorce from her husband, Bain had adamantly refused. To McKelvey, the motive was that the two lovers plotted the murder to free themselves of Bain so that they might have a life of their own.

The witnesses for the prosecution basically told of finding the body, questioning the two who were indicted and having seen the two together in public. The prosecution's witnesses also talked of Parker having a revolver. Again it was noted that the two had been seen in establishments that sold alcohol but no witness testified of their imbibing.

In an effort to show that Bain was not abusive and really cared for his wife, the prosecution put on the stand a local merchant. The man told of Bain purchasing a silk dress and other personal items for Elizabeth. At first the man said that this was in 1916, which was when the couple was separated, but under cross-examination recanted his statement saying the incident was in 1915, which would have made it right after the couple reconciled.

Defense

The couple's presence in the courtroom sent mixed messages. Robert Parker looked like a young man anyone would want to have has a neighbor. His demeanor was humble and responsible. Even at a trial where her life was in jeopardy, Elizabeth's natural alluring beauty was noticed. She was the woman that if she moved in next door, wives may suddenly find their husbands enjoying yard work.

At the time of this case adultery was a criminal offense. Toohey knew he had to tackle the moral and criminal aspects of Parker's and Elizabeth's relationship. In his opening statement he addressed the illicit nature of the relationship by trying to pass along the blame for their intimacy. Toohey said the intimacy, or as he put it, "Mrs. Bain's waywardness," was the result of three contributing factors. First and foremost were the extremely poor conditions of her home life both with her mother and with Peter

Ransom Bain. Second, and not far behind, was the example set by her father (who was conveniently dead). Third, was Peter Ransom Bain himself who Toohey characterized as fundamentally worthless. According to Toohey, Bain's worthlessness was both as a husband and a citizen in general so his wife sought the company of a stable man.

There were three witnesses that talked about Ransom Bain's behavior. One was the proprietor of a local hotel who testified to frequently selling Bain hard liquor. The second was the usher at the moving picture theater who testified about how frequently, when Parker and Elizabeth were at the theater, he would see Bain hanging around outside. The third man had the most condemning testimony. Chester Duel was a handyman at the Marshal place. Chester testified that on one occasion he had caught Bain trying to get into his wife's room through a window. The handyman had chased Bain away with an axe. Chester had a bad stuttering problem and the pressure of being in court did not help. Under cross-examination, McKelvey asked Chester if he had ever drank, meaning of course, hard liquor. Chester's reply added levity to the otherwise tense trial when he said, "I never had but three glasses of birch beer in my life."

One of the heart wrenching witnesses for the defense was Elizabeth's mother, Cora Durling. Cora, who had remarried, told of the problems she had faced because of her first husband, Elizabeth's father. She told the court how Elizabeth's natural father was an intemperate man. With prohibition on everyone's mind, blaming social and family ills on the curses of alcohol was a smart move by a defense attorney. According to Mrs. Durling, because of her first husband's habits she was forced to take hard jobs working alongside men just to keep food on the table and a roof over the head of her litter. She told how when Elizabeth was only a child she had been required to work alongside of her mother in the fields.

In front of an emotion filled courtroom, Cora took responsibility for the marriage of her daughter. She told the jury that the first she ever met Peter Ransom Bain was when he came to her house and asked for her daughter's hand in marriage. She said it was her idea for the Elizabeth to get married so young (Elizabeth was only 15 when Bain asked for her hand. She turned 16 on August 2, a mere two months before the marriage). Cora said that she had been led to believe that Bain had some money and would be a good provider. In hindsight, Cora felt she was misled by Bain.

Cora told the jury how by the middle of March, after her daughter's November wedding, Elizabeth was home three times a week just to get food for herself. This was during the period when Bain worked at the Todd Farm and before Elizabeth took the job at the hotel at Cossayuna Lake. Cora went on to say that when she visited Elizabeth during that period there had been no food in her daughter's home. Exactly how Bain was spending his $26 salary is not clear, but it is evident he was not spending it on his wife's necessities.

Both of the two reconciliations between Elizabeth and Bain had been at Cora's urging. At the second and final reconciliation, Cora believed that Bain had finally learned his lesson and wanted to provide for Elizabeth. It is unfair to comment ninety-years after about the feelings that people may have had for each other. In fairness, Bain had waited until a relatively mature age to marry. In contrast, he had selected a bride much younger than he. One could argue, as the prosecution did, that he loved and wanted to provide for his young wife. Or one could take the position of the defense that he was possessive and wanted to control Elizabeth, not provide for her.

The strength of Cora's testimony came not only from her words but also from her presence. She was absolutely tiny. She was so small that when she talked of the hard work she had been expected to perform on behalf of her children, everyone's heart went out to her. The weakness in Cora's testimony came when, on cross-examination, she stated that regardless of how poor the Bain's home had been, she thought Elizabeth was "happier" when she was with Ransom.

Parker's father was also a witness. Although he could add nothing to the facts in the case, he did add emotion. The old man spoke at length and through tears about the type of man he had raised his son to be. He talked of how Parker was responsible, had worked hard and in the same place (not needing to change jobs as Bain had done). Old Man Parker had tears on his cheek as he testified to his son's character. Young Parker, through his hard work, had provided for his father. To Old Man Parker, the most important fact was that his son had never before been in trouble.

Henry Parker went on to tell that on the night of the fire his son had woken him to tell him about the fight and that he had killed Bain. When the "old man" asked why, his son had said, "I had to; it was Bain or I."

Two witnesses were put on the stand from Bald Mountain. Both of these witness testified that Bain had said that the issues between he and Parker had reached a point where his (Bain's) jealousy was out of control. To each of these witnesses, Bain had said words to the effect, "I am going down there and see this thing out. It may be life or death an' I hope it will be me."

The only other significant defense witness was Elizabeth's employer, Mrs. Walker. Mrs. Walker told how she had caught Bain cutting the screen to Elizabeth's window in an effort to break into her room.

The defendants as witnesses

The defense was desperate. Despite their arguments, the judge had admitted the statements made by Parker and Elizabeth the day after the fire. In an effort to mitigate the effects of these statements, Toohey placed Parker on the stand.

The packed courtroom was absolutely silent as Parker testified. Parker, who was pale from the strain, could not contradict what had been recognized. Parker did try to establish that, despite the words that had been written in the statements, on the night of the fight he was in fact worried about his own and Elizabeth's safety when they were confronted by Bain. Parker went on to explain that the statements were made after a sleepless night. He also stressed to the jury that some parts of what he had said were not recorded.

Although he shifted in the witness chair, Parker seemed sincere when he said that the unsigned letter was meant to set up a meeting to discuss divorce. He testified that the requested meeting had happened at the Marshal house a few days after the letter went out and three weeks before the assault.

When Parker described the fight he was animated. His hands made bold gestures as if reenacting those fateful moments.

For the two and a half hours that Parker was on the stand, he maintained a solid, if low, voice. The entire time Parker testified he gazed only at the jury, his attorney and the judge. He never looked at Elizabeth. To all present he seemed genuine and there was a prevailing feeling that Rob had done as well for himself as could have been expected under the circumstances.

Finally, it was Elizabeth's turn to be on the stand. The crowd had waited to hear the words of the woman who had held the hearts of two men so closely that one would kill and the other die just to be with her.

On the stand she impressed everyone with her posture and her presence. She sat like a woman in control, holding herself as if she intended to give all present a clear view. Her voice was so loud that it almost resonated off the walls of the courtroom. Her testimony took an hour and three quarters. Like her mother, she told of her childhood and having to work instead of attending school. She confirmed that the meeting requested in the unsigned letter had happened the next week in front of the Marshal house, but that Bain had refused to agree to let her have a divorce.

Where Parker had been able to appear cool under cross-examination, Elizabeth was nervous. She became irritable when asked about what she meant about being too much of a "sport" for her husband. At this time, sporting men were another name for gamblers and men who lived the fast life. The women they traveled with may have had fun, but it was usually perceived these women lived an immoral life. Elizabeth said that when she used the word "sport" she meant that she liked "to go to the moving pictures" and "other places to have a good time" in the evening.

It was generally believed that Elizabeth did not do as well as Parker up to this point, but it was one of her last answers that she inevitably regretted the most. When asked about why she had told Bain to stay away from the Marshal house, she said it was because she did not "want him shot on the premises." Even her affirmative answer to Toohey's question on redirect, where he asked her if what she meant to say was that she didn't want him shot anywhere, failed to take the sting out of the words.

The testimony in the trial ended with two questions asked

of Elizabeth by Toohey. First he asked, "Did you directly or indirectly cause Ransom Bain to come where you were that night?"

To which Elizabeth replied, "No, indeed."

Toohey then asked, "Did you at any time plan to kill Ransom Bain?"

Her answer was the same, "No, indeed."

Closing Arguments

In their closing arguments, the Defense also took aim directly at the Bain family. In words that would be considered clearly politically incorrect today, Toohey reminded the jury of the appearance of two of Bain's brothers who had attended the trial. Toohey also held up a picture of Ransom and asked how any young girl of sixteen could be expected to spend a winter with these three men (Bain and his brothers).

Toohey played heavily on Elizabeth's youth at the time of her marriage and her poverty. He also tried to build support for the character of Parker. The problem was that he walked a delicate line because if he made Parker look too good that would only mean that he was pulled into this relationship by a temptress (Elizabeth).

Toohey also raised the issue of the statements taken without benefit of an attorney. Listening to Toohey's explanation of his clients and their lives for the first time at the trial, Parker broke down with tears streaming down his face. Whether the results of Toohey's words or whether it was tide of emotions, the courtroom became a sea of white as the spectators pulled out their handkerchiefs to absorb the tears that ran off the faces of many in the courtroom.

One of the key issues was premeditation. Toohey tried to bury this issue when he acknowledged that Parker had a gun. Toohey asked the jury, "Would a man plan a murder and then not use the gun he had carried in public?"

All in all, Toohey received very high marks for his closing.

McKelvey could see what he was up against. The district attorney tried to push back the emotions that Toohey had so brazenly awakened in the room. McKelvey reminded the jury that they were "here to determine the guilt or innocence of the defendants and not to indulge in weeping and wailing and the gnashing of teeth." At another point he told the jurors that he had done what he should do for the law and that they should do the same. To McKelvey, duty meant not allowing feelings to interfere with justice.

The jury has a problem

This case presented Saratoga County and perhaps the jurisprudence system throughout the nation with a problem that had not been previously faced. It was the practice in Saratoga County to sequester juries in Capital cases. This jury, like those before it, was housed during the period of the trial in one of the hotels in Ballston Spa. In the days before television or radio, the sheriffs' deputies would take the jury members to events to make their stay more comfortable and at the same time less confining. To assure a fair trial, the deputies were responsible for guaranteeing that no one involved in the case had contact with any member of the jury. As a result of the Billing's trial, where it was learned that some men on the jury went to play pool, or worse yet, were seen dancing, the deputies were in charge of setting up "respectable" entertainment. The night before the case closed the jury went to see "a moving picture." The movie that was selected by the deputy was entitled "The Eye of God," a title that seemed appropriate. The story line was not what the prosecutor would have wanted any jury to see. The film told the story of a jury confronted by a man charged with murder. They hear the case and convict the man sending him to prison for life. Twenty years later, a second man on his deathbed confesses to the murder. It was an emotional movie meant to question the jury system.

When the Judge heard about the theme of the movie, he wondered if the jury may have been tainted. Judge Whitmyer asked each juror if he felt that seeing the movie would hinder him from making a judgment based on the evidence in this case. Each man said "no" and the judge ruled that the case could continue. It is impossible to see into the mind of another person; however, the ultimate verdict in this case may very well have been influenced by the movie the jury saw the night before they had to render their own verdict.

The Verdict

The jury deliberated for only three hours bringing in their verdict at 6:00 pm. It was the dinner hour and no one expected that they would reach a decision so quickly. Virtually everyone in attendance that day had gone home or to a restaurant for their evening meal. The only ones who had stayed through were Elizabeth's mother, Cora Durling; Robert's father, Henry Parker; and a few reporters who had covered the situation since its inception the previous July 23. Between the time the jury, through a deputy sheriff, informed the judge that they had arrived at a verdict and the time the court officially reconvened, the news that there was a verdict had spread throughout Ballston Spa. As the jury came back into the courtroom, there were a number of spectators in attendance. The scene was well attended but sparse by comparison to when Parker and Elizabeth had testified the previous afternoon.

The jury found the two guilty of manslaughter in the first degree. When the verdict was read Robert Parker and Elizabeth Bain showed little emotion. In contrast, their parents Cora Stover Durling and Henry Parker, both broke down in court. The law required a two day waiting period before a sentence was pronounced. Both the prosecution and the defense waived the traditional waiting period. As if understanding the gravity of the situation, the young couple held hands. This was one of the few exhibitions of affection that they had shown during the entire trial.

The in the dark of late fall evening, the pair were sentenced to a minimum of 10 or a maximum of 19 years six months. It was the most severe sentence the judge could have issued for a conviction on a charge of manslaughter.

Upon hearing her fate, tears could be seen in Elizabeth's eyes; Parker held back his emotion. Their families gathered around the convicted lovers for the last time. The two kissed each of their supporters in turn, and then were led from the court to begin their sentence.

Elizabeth and Parker each served almost exactly the ten years, being released just months before attorney Toohey's untimely death of a heart attack in 1926. Their parents had died while they were in prison.

Parker returned to Schuylerville and worked in a mill; he never married. No record could be found of what became of Elizabeth.

The site where the assault happened was 500 feet north of the B & M train station in Schuylerville. The station is near a museum that can be seen on the north side of Route 29. The building is just west of the Schuylerville schools. The actual site of the Chubb Barn and the assault would be on what are now the playing fields of the School.

There was yet another tragedy of a far greater magnitude than Bain's death that was reported in the newspapers the same time as the fire.

Nineteen-year-old Cora Pratt had been wading with three friends when she went out too far from shore and fell off a deep drop-off in the Hoosick River. Her friend, thirteen-year old Alice Morrison, and her sister, fifteen-year-old Ada, tried to help. Like Cora, their clothes became soaked with water and pulled them down.

Two men heard the screams and rushed to help. The men were able to pull the girls from the river but were unable to resuscitate any of them.

So much for the idea that the long skirts of the era protected one's daughter.

Florence Bussey

"You're running after my husband!"

The employees who worked the front desk of the Whitcomb House in Rochester were milling around completing the variety of tasks that kept them occupied in the midday. The hotel's personnel were as always, busy, very busy, but not in the same ways as people who work the front desk of hotels are occupied today. It was the mid 1880s, there were no computers, telephones, automated check in or magnetic door locks to change. There were, however, carriages arriving, guests to be checked in and baggage to be carried upstairs. Unlike today, each guest had to be registered individually while standing at the counter. New guests had to provide either letters of credit or leave a cash deposit to cover projected expenses. As in most hotels of the day, guests signed for purchases and these charges were then checked by an individual and added to the person's account. Keeping track of all the paper required a front desk staff much larger than those in hotels today.

Added to the mundane accounting tasks were the responsibilities of maintaining the lobby. In these busy times the lobby of a hotel had an entirely different personality than those of even the finest hotels today. The lobby was the place where everyone in the hotel gathered to socialize. For those who didn't want to talk with other guests, it was a place to read the newspapers, write letters or just smoke a cigar. Like all the great "houses" of the period, the first floor of the Whitcomb House consisted of lounges, the main lobby and restaurants. Even though there were elevators in existence, most people still had to walk up at least one flight of stairs to reach the first level that had accommodations.

Suddenly, there was a sound that was described as a loud crack. Those at the desk looked at each other, an expression of uncertainty on their faces. Had they taken the time to confer, the employees would all agree that the sound they heard was extremely similar to the report of a gunshot. Such things were just not expected to happen in the suites of the ultra exclusive

Whitcomb House. People at this hotel paid for service and security, not scandal and disturbances. Successful men might check into the hotel accompanied by one of their "nieces," but violence or the creation of a scene was simply not acceptable.

The leaders, either naturally or by position, hesitated only momentarily before they ran upstairs in search of the source of the sound. When the employees reached the first floor that housed guestrooms, it was determined that the sound had emanated in Suite 19. This conclusion was easy to reach as conveniently, the door to the room had been left open and the residue of gun smoke could be smelled wafting from the room. The open door allowed the inquisitive employees to look in without feeling like they were intruding. What they witnessed amazed this group of sophisticated service workers. On the stylish carpet lay an elegantly dressed woman sobbing hysterically. On each finger of the desperate woman's hands were expensive rings. Each ring had one or more precious gems set in a band of gold or silver. At first glance the prostrate woman, who was weeping uncontrollably, met all the criteria of a true Victorian lady. To the cynical employees, she was the type who met the necessary standards to be classified as the spoiled wife.

As they entered the room, the staff could see a second woman kneeling over the evidently "fine lady." The second woman was nursing the screaming woman, talking serenely trying to reassure and calm the lady's hysteria. The second woman was also well dressed but not quite as finely dressed as the frantic woman.

Those on the staff of the Whitcomb House were skilled at judging people by there clothes, language and attitude. To do their job proficiently, the staff could make accurate assessments of people with little more than a glance. Automatically, they used their intuitive skills on the second woman. Her clothes were less expensive and she had none of the jeweled accessories adorning her hands. To them, this second woman was not dressed cheaply but neither was she dressed in the full regalia that the staff had seen on many of their guests. She did not fit any of the hotel's stereotypes. The woman who was attending to the screaming lady was young and beautiful. Women who met this description, and came to this hotel, were usually the wives or "nieces" of the men who had rented the room. But if she was the "friend of a guest," why wasn't she wearing better clothes and at least some jewelry? She was an anomaly to the staff and would later prove to be dilemma for the media.

After making their social evaluations, it would have been impossible for the staff not to notice that the woman caring for the prostrate woman had a blood escaping from her forehead. The cause of the blood was apparent; to the side of the prostrate woman was a pearl handled 22-calibre derringer lying on the floorboards. It was quickly surmised that the woman caring for the sobbing woman was, in fact, suffering from a gunshot wound. *The only plausible explanation was that the wounded woman was taking care of the woman who had shot her only moments before*. A scene such as what was playing out before the staff would have been unusual anywhere, but in the Whitcomb House this was extraordinary.

The Media

It was late in the morning when the shooting took place. The reporters from the local newspapers knew that if they hurried they could file a story just in time for the late afternoon editions. Just like today, it was important to a reporter's career to be the first to break a story. *The Rochester Daily* that afternoon carried the headline "**Love And Jealousy.**" Because of the social significance of the principals involved, by the next day the newspapers around the state were loaded with headlines such as "**A Troy Wife Shoots Her Husband's Mistress**," "**Another Tragedy**" and "**A Mysterious Affair**." None of these early headlines captured the magnitude of the case that was slowly unfolding. It is worth noting that many newspapers, especially those attempting to be upscale, used the term "tragedy" whenever a shooting or other attempted murder occurred.

An intriguing story

From the first newspaper coverage of this engaging story, the screaming woman would be correctly acknowledged as "the wife." The wounded woman would prove to be much harder to identify. In the first reports, she was portrayed as the husband's mistress. Later her role would change almost as often as the speculation of her name.

Any of the experienced staff at the Whitcomb House would have questioned the newspapers' characterization of the second woman as a mistress. But then, reporters are not sophisticated service staff. In fact, reporters and elite service staff respond to people in very different ways. To have an exclusive, reporters will not share with each other, but they will tell the general public. Good service workers work in the converse; they will talk to each other but never divulge what they know or believe about a person to anyone outside their own group. Reporters are better at questioning the truthfulness of people, while service staff members succeed by assuming everyone is misrepresenting him or herself.

The failure to identify the wounded woman properly was the first fault in reports of the incident that were to unfold. To make matters even more complicated, it wasn't the reporters' fault that they could not get the story correct. Literally everyone who was involved in this twisted tale wanted what had occurred to be kept as quiet as possible; that is, except one lady who had not yet been introduced. Luckily for the anxious reporters assigned to cover the unfolding events in this case, there was that one other woman who wanted the *(her)* story told.

Mistake

The first night it was confirmed that when she pulled the trigger, the lady had intended to shoot her husband's mistress. It would be twenty-four hours before it was learned that a terrible mistake had been made. The woman who had been shot was not the woman the wife believed to be her husband's mistress. The shooting of the wrong woman was only the first twist in this convoluted tale. Before it was settled the story would have more turns before the flame that it ignited would slowly die out and the embers disappear for a hundred years.

Keeping track or who was who

Because of the husband's perceived sexual dalliances, and those of one of the ladies in this story, it took a scorecard for the reporters and readers to keep track of the players. However, because the status of those involved covered the entire social spectrum, everyone in Rochester, Troy and all the points in between were ready and willing to keep a scorecard.

As time progressed, this story would cut across all classes, linking a series of individuals whose lives would never have been assumed to intertwine. The entire gamut of Victorian society was transected in this one tale including; those in the working poor to those with extreme wealth; two divorcees to a refined wife; a Victorian gentleman to philandering son; the owner of a large mill to a bartender and an unemployed mill hand. The newspaper readers would all agree it would be hard to imagine a better story even from a novelist.

The breadth of this case could also be measured in geographical terms. It crossed the life of a woman of the highest social (although perhaps not moral and definitely not emotional) standing from Moline, Illinois, with people from Troy, Rochester, Saratoga Springs and Perry, New York.

The motivation for this assault is not difficult to establish. What was not understood for several days is that the circumstances that provoked this shooting began at least two years before and not in Rochester, but in Troy. What is equally interesting is the ultimate outcome of the events regarding the husband's career.

What being from Troy meant

The lady who was discovered laying prostrate on the floor was Florence Bussey (the wife). At the time of the shooting, the Bussey family was one of the wealthiest in Troy. This classification in itself was a major feat as, during the Victorian Era, Troy was one of the leading industrial and financial centers in America. A large part of Troy's economic dominance was based on its location. Troy's industry started because of a series of waterfalls in the area. These waterfalls were harnessed for energy to turn the saws, grindstones and lathes of early industries. Unlike other places that had waterfalls, Troy also had access to the Hudson River for transportation of raw goods and finished products. Later, when the canals were finished, the fact that Troy was almost exactly at the junction of the Erie Canal and the Hudson River spurred even more growth in the city. The Erie Canal was at that time the major transportation link between the agricultural west and the industrial northeast. The other important source of much of the community's wealth was the efforts of one man, Russell Sage. Sage was a financial wizard who had built himself an empire and helped transform his native city of Troy into one of America's economic centers. He was also the man after whom the women's college was named.

The Busseys and their fortune

Esek Bussey, Florence's father-in-law, was the principle partner in one of the large iron foundries located in Troy. Bussey's company was a classic example of the right firm, at the right time, led by the right man. The headquarters of Bussey and McLeod Stove Works was located on Oakwood Avenue. The forging plant, which employed 400 workers, was in what was referred to as the hill section. This story takes place in 1884, the era of coal and wood stoves. These valuable appliances had, in one hundred years, helped transform American homes from cold, damp hovels, heated inefficiently by fireplaces, into reasonably warm spaces centered around the kitchen. A large part of the credit for this social transformation is found in the work and patents of Esek Bussey.

Esek Bussey was born in 1826, in the small community of Hoosick Falls, near the Vermont border with New York. When Esek was eleven, his family moved into the city of Troy where his father, Col. Thomas Bussey, took over as the proprietor of the Northern Hotel. From a very young age Esek had a taste for business. He began his career working at the corner grocery store. This was not just any corner store, this store was owned by Russell Sage, the soon to be financier. Throughout Esek's life he would remark proudly about his relationship with Sage. Esek did leave Troy for a period while a teenager, moving to Central New York. He had returned to his adopted home by the time he was in his early twenties and was a resident of the city for the rest of his life.

Esek Bussey's first entrepreneurial establishment was a combination retail hardware store and tin shop. Young and under financed, he rented out part of his display space to Charles McLeod, who owned a small wood molding firm. McCloud's firm produced the wooden molds on which thin metal was placed then hammered into the desired shape. In partnership with McLeod, Bussey successfully won the bid to put a tin roof on the new

Union Train Station in Troy. It was a natural partnership with one man, McLeod, skilled in putting in the struts and frame and the other, Bussey, in installing the final metal roof.

By the time the workmen had finished the station project, the two partners realized that their professional relationship could be the foundation for an effective business team. With the profits from the major project (the station), the two men then set up a new company manufacturing pots, pans and other stove utensils. The production of cooking utensils was straight forward with little creativity either required or desired. In 1859, the firm of Bussey and McLeod made the transition from producing utensils to the manufacturing of wood stoves. It was in the manufacturing of stoves that Esek Bussey demonstrated his real genius. Over the course of the next fifty years, Esek would be credited with many patents and improvements in the design and operations of stoves.

One of the most important inventions attributed to Bussey was the hot water reservoir inside his woodstoves. Today, we take for granted what our ancestors considered chores. In the 1800s there was no such thing as hot water on demand. At the end of America's Revolution, to clean or wash clothes, dishes or themselves, people had to heat water in a pot or kettle over an open fire. Later, with the arrival of the wood stove, it became easier to heat water on the stove surface but it was still a task. Hot water still required filling a pot and waiting for the water to heat, which required planning. With the advent of woodstoves, inventors tried to find ways to have hot water more readily available. One of the first ideas tried was to provide hot water by installing a tank around the stovepipe. Heating water by way of a reservoir around the pipe at first appeared to be a logical solution to the problem of a ready source of hot water. The use of the vent seemed to be efficient, as it was generally believed that too much heat escaped up the chimney. Although adding convenience, the tanks were difficult to fill without burning ones knuckles on the hot pipe. An additional problem was that the water would, over time, either drain or evaporate. When the metal exhaust pipe, which usually held water, was exposed to air, it inevitably rusted. These rusted pipes caused fires. Seeing the faults in this system, Esek designed a reservoir built into the side of the stove from which hot water could be dipped at any time. So successful was his invention that other manufactures paid over $150,000 in royalties to incorporate the Bussey system in their stoves.

Other inventions credited to Esek were a double fire pot stove (which provided a more even heat surface) and improvements to the dampers installed in the pipes (this greatly improved the efficiency of the stoves). A real aide to older people and women was Esek's self-feeder stoves (stoves where the wood was stored on the side before entering the fire box). With the self-feeder stove, wood could be stored for hours. Finally, those who stayed at home each day did not need to lift heavy logs into the firebox while the stronger family members were at work.

So successful was the Bussey stove firm that as Americans moved west, Bussey set up a second operation known as The Chicago Stove Works. Unfortunately, the Chicago factory burned in the great fire of 1872. Undaunted by the loss of the Chicago works, Bussey rebuilt the factory and the family's fortunes continued to grow.

Philanthropy

There are many stories about Esek and how he used his wealth. A large part of America's industrial revolution was supported by the Calvinist philosophy of giving. Simply said, if one gave to those less fortunate in their community or to their church, they would ultimately be rewarded. The advantage of adopting this philosophy was that it was often believed that the reward would occur while the person was still alive. One example of this belief in action was the report of one specific financial contribution made by Esek. Troy was becoming a true city and as such had decided to end the annual mud problems resulting from unpaved streets and walkways. When the United Presbyterian Church on Fifth Avenue in Troy learned it was to be assessed by the city for the cost of a sidewalk, the church officials felt they did not have the resources to meet the cost. By the time of the church's sidewalk concern, Esek was already considered to be a local philanthropist. At the church council's meeting he agreed to personally pay the full cost of installing the sidewalk. On his way home from that council meeting, Esek's creative mind developed the ides for an oven shelf that would lower and rise as the door was opened or closed. By lowering when the door was closed and rising when the door was opened, it meant the user did not have to bend over as far to place items into the oven. Royalties on this one invention were said to have paid the church's sidewalk assessment many times over.

Esek also funded a fire company in the hill section of Troy, which was named in his honor. It should be noted that Esek was not entirely altruistic in his gift giving: the fire company he created was responsible for protecting the Bussey's home and business.

The Bussey Family & Harry

In 1848, Esek Bussey married Cornelia Cruikshank. The couple had one daughter, Cornelia, who married and lived in Chicago. They also had four sons; James, who ran a branch of the family business in Colorado; William, who watched out for the family's interest in Chicago; Esek Jr., who stayed in Troy to help his father; and Thomas Henry, called "Harry," who is the center of this story. It could be reasonably said that as his brothers were devoted caretakers of the family's interest in different places in the United States, Harry was equally diligent in watching out for his own interests, especially if those interests happened to be female.

Harry Bussey, perhaps because he was spoiled, or more likely because it would have been his nature no matter what his status at birth, lived, what in the Victorian Era was referred to as, 'the fast life.' It was not that Harry did not work; before he was thirty he had held several managerial positions both in his father's factory and at manufacturing operations owned by his father's friends in the Troy region. The conjecture that Harry lived the "fast life" was based on his lifestyle, especially when he was out on the town. Harry enjoyed the company of women, the taste of good spirits, and the risk of a sporting wager. If maintained in a temperate way, these were accepted traits in successful men in Victorian society. Harry's problem was that, during this period in his life, he wasn't moderate in his vices.

In an effort to either control Harry or at least have him out of the family's sight, for a period in the late 1870s, his father had him assigned to work at one of the family's business interests in Chicago.

Eventually, Esek tired of Harry's conduct and encouraged him to marry. To ensure social status, the wealthy Florence Wilson was selected to be his wife. Florence was from Chicago but had lived in of Moline, Illinois for close to a decade. The connection of the Wilson and Bussey families was the result of the Bussey's businesses in Chicago.

Florence Wilson Bussey

Despite the Bussey family's desire and expectation that their son marry well, Florence Wilson proved to be somewhat of a tarnished angel in her own right. Florence had been born and raised in Chicago, Illinois. Later, her family moved to Moline where, as a teenager, her life was characterized as having the "ups and downs of a society belle." As a young socialite, Flo, as she was affectionately called by her many admirers, was coquettish. She was such a skilled flirt that her behavior was characterized as being "fond of company." This term is close to, but not nearly as bad as, the male equivalent "fast company." Living in Moline for over ten years, Florence had earned a reputation for being "as well known" as any woman in the community. As a rising debutant, she was pampered and her good looks both helped and hurt her socially. In a time when many people only owned one or two outfits, Florence was recognized for being as well dressed as anyone in her community. Of all her personality and physical traits, it was her pale complexion that is mentioned as a primary descriptor throughout her life. Her skin was so light in color that it appeared almost transparent.

Before becoming the wife of Harry Bussey, Florence had been married to DeWitte Dimock, also from Moline. Florence was only a teenager at the time of her first wedding and Dimock was twenty years her senior. The Dimock marriage took place in February of 1871. So grand was the event that it was considered to be one of the principle social events of Moline that winter. On the surface, by marrying Dimock, Florence was considered to have married well; after all he had relatives that were considered, by Moline standards, to be prosperous. One of the best examples of Dimock's family's wealth was one of her wedding presents. An uncle of DeWitte's had built and furnished a cottage for the couple to live in.

For four years the wedding cottage served as the social center for both husband and wife. The parties in this house epitomized their generation's desire for friends and entertainment. In their cottage, the couple frequently entertained the best of Moline's society. By 1878 the marriage seemed to have faltered. Both parties felt the other was responsible. DeWitte described his home relations as having "grown cold." Naturally, Florence blamed her husband for the breakdown in the relationship. It would be impossible to determine the true causes; however, Dimock took up an "independent life style." In simple words, he began "keeping company" with other women.

In 1878, DeWitte successfully ran for clerk of the city. Almost immediately after the election he took up residence in his own apartment. Florence suited for divorce on the grounds of adultery. During the divorce process Florence stayed on in Moline maintaining appearances by having her widowed mother move in with her in the wedding cottage.

When the divorce suit went into court a few months after the election, DeWitte never even showed up to defend himself. When the divorce was final and she was again legally single, Florence returned to her maiden name of Wilson and moved with her mother back to Chicago where she could put the unpleasant marriage behind her and once again become a socialite.

At the very least, Florence was considered to be pleasant in appearance. Most newspaper reports in the days that followed assured their readers that she was attractive. Florence had light brown hair and always dressed fashionably. Her most noted physical attribute, other than her pale skin, was her extremely light blue eyes. Some attributed the paleness of the skin to the stress that had existed in her first marriage, especially during the period of 1875-78. Anything she may have lacked in looks (which is doubtful) was made up for in style, grace and glamour. After her divorce and before her second marriage it was well known that Florence had several admirers. During this period, at parties and other socially occasions she was considered to be "lively."

Florence, however, also had her shortcomings. Not one for moderation, her faults were not downsides, they were sheer cliffs.

Florence Wilson had the tendency to throw tantrums which were only matched by her fits of jealousy. Her predisposition toward anger was combined with an impulsive temperament forming a blend in social behavior equivalent to the chemical reactions of nitrogen and glycerin. Victorian society had terms that were less direct and more stylish than those used today. *The New York World* described her as "when excited capable of showing much temper."

When Florence met Harry Bussey it looked like a match of social equals.

Florence and Harry

In 1880, the Wilson family and the Bussey family were joined. Soon after their Chicago marriage the couple moved to Troy, a change that was projected help both of them socially. They took up residence with Esek and Cornelia in the Bussey's family estate. In Troy, Florence was rewarded with the opportunity to start over in yet unexplored social circles; perhaps now people would stop whispering about her past. On the other hand, hopefully she could stop showing her anger. With Harry a married man, it was assumed that the return to his family base would signal he had resolved his social behaviors.

There was little reason for optimism. Even after he married, there is little indication that Harry's social conduct altered significantly. There is even less proof the Flo's temper improved and there is no evidence that she became less jealous.

With birth certificates not issued until 1882, the exact ages of Harry and Florence are hard to determine. In all probability, the difficulty is because she was older than he and did not want to share that information. It appears that in 1884, at the time of the shooting in Rochester, Harry was about 29. Florence had married for the first time thirteen years before in 1871. Even assuming she was around eighteen when she married the first time, this would have made her 30 or 31 when the tragedy in the Whitcomb House occurred. One newspaper carried her age as 22, which is probably a full 10 years younger than her actual age.

Enough is enough

The marriage and return to Troy proved to have a dark side. Almost immediately after Harry and Florence arrived in Troy it was rumored that he had resumed the "fast life." The proof was when Harry's name again appeared as the correspondent in a divorce proceeding.

Becoming exasperated by his son's behavior, in January of 1884, Esek set Harry up to be the superintendent of a textile factory in Perry, New York. Perry is a small community south of Rochester. Before Harry left for Perry, his father told him that this was his last chance. Esek told his wayward son in no uncertain terms that if he could not improve his conduct with the move to Perry, he would not be welcome in the Bussey's family home in the future. As events would soon indicate, Esek's lecture and threat did not rectify Harry's social flaws.

A Fresh Start

Relocating to Perry was received by the younger Busseys as a combination of blessing and condemnation; while Esek considered Perry the prefect option. On the up side, the mill in question was an opportunity for Harry to set up his own business and become recognized in his own right as a businessman. On the down side, Perry was a small village with a limited social circle. Harry and Flo were used to the amenities of city life available in Chicago and Troy.

Harry believed that the move to Western New York would yield one advantage; he would no longer be stuck in the immense shadow of his father. Esek Bussey had a hard earned reputation, status, and respect. In Troy, the Bussey name carried with it an image that Harry had found difficult to avoid. The move to Perry might eliminate some of the pressure he felt to be perfect.

Esek believed that in Perry many of his son's social temptation should be removed, thus this move was the remedy for the family's ailments. Esek was a man used to being in control. It mattered little to him if the relocation did not suit the desires and lifestyles of those making the move.

The plan was that the Bussey's money would be infused into a struggling textile mill in Perry creating a partnership with the Bussey family holding the majority share. Esek was a shrewd businessman, so the negotiations for the sale took several days. The sale was finally completed in the days just before Harry left for Perry. After the negotiation ended and before the move, Harry went to New York City to purchase equipment necessary to improve the factory and make the factory more efficient. After the shooting, there would be a major debate about what occurred on this trip.

It was well established that Harry left by train late in the afternoon; the sale was final. It was also understood that Harry spent the night in New York City. The next day he went from the City to Providence, Rhode Island then returned to Troy the evening of the second day. The disagreement would focus on whether Harry had company for at least a portion of this excursion.

After the shooting, the rumor mill in Troy thrived like a raging fire. The rumor that dominated the communication among neighbors was that the woman that Flo had meant to shoot had accompanied Harry to New York City on his fateful business trip.

Morality, media and circulation

The perception that during the Victorian era people lived a more moral life, resulting in only limited social scandals, is simply not true. One only needs to read the old newspapers carefully to see that there were carefully worded expressions used as a mask to cover obvious troubles and double standards.

It was only by chance that it would be in the Whitcomb House that the events of this story ultimately unfolded. At the same time, the fact that it did happen in such an upscale hotel added to the story line; after all, the a shooting by a woman in one of the city's most exclusive hotels smelled of scandal.

Newspapers then, as now, lived on circulation. Gossip and tragedy sold newspapers. This story had both a shooting and the roots of a scandal; thus, it was apparent that there would be an economic windfall to the newspaper with the first and the best story. Being first meant more readers and more sales. Under this intense pressure, reporters found that even more important than accuracy was having a story printed in the same day's afternoon editions. Sex rumors or not, some of the Rochester newspapers wanted to be sure they had the story at least somewhat correct.

It had been approximately half past eleven in the morning when the woman who was shot had arrived at the hotel. The time of the shooting meant that shortcuts had to be taken if the story would be in the afternoon editions. In fairness, the reporters failed in accuracy primarily because the woman who was shot would not talk to officials, let alone the press. Without her statement they had to write about what they witnessed or heard, even if it was not credible.

The story unfolds

After the hotel staff investigated the source of the shot, a bellboy was sent to find a police officer. It had been approximately ten minutes between the time of the shot and the arrival of the first officer at the scene. By the time the officer got to the hotel, he found the crime scene totally disturbed. Among the changes that had been made was the movement of the wounded woman to an unoccupied room.

The officer went down the hall to look in on the injured woman. He found that Dr. Harrington was already tending to her wound. The doctor had removed a small ball from just below the skin of her forehead and was stitching up her abrasion. Asked by the police officer for information, the wounded woman refused to give any particulars regarding the incident. She would not even provide her name. Her self imposed silence would frustrate the investigation and intrigue the press and its readers. Trying to brush aside the incident, the wounded woman told the officer that she wanted nothing done regarding being having been shot.

The media shows up

At least two reporters were at the hotel while everyone involved was still present. By the time the first reporter saw the shooting victim, she had already pulled a small lock of hair from beneath her bonnet to cover the wound. The reporters on the scene gave a description of the wounded woman that was similar to the numerous others that were to follow. She was described as being "quite pretty." Later reports on her appearance, if anything, added to the perception that the wounded woman was extremely attractive. She was uniformly described as being of medium height and "luxuriously formed." These candid descriptors added to the perception that the wounded woman had to be Harry's mistress; such words would not have been used with respect to a legitimate lady.

One reporter at the hotel noted that the wounded woman went so far as to refuse to go the police station with the first officer on the scene. It was the second officer who arrived at the hotel that was able to convince the wounded woman to go to the station to make a statement. Her agreement, however, was contingent on her being accompanied by the doctor who had been treating her. Although it is not clear why the wounded woman wanted the doctor to be with her, it is known that particles of the spent black powder were embedded in her eyes. She may have still felt the potential existed for further medical assistance. It may have also been that the doctor was the only person who had treated her kindly since she entered the hotel.

Exactly when or how the Rochester Police became aware of the influence wielded by the people involved in this case is not certain. The officers may have assumed some wealth based on the fact that one of the parties had a suite at such an exclusive hotel. It is equally possible that an officer had been cautioned by one of the employees of the hotel. What is certain is that there were indications of the political connections noted as soon as the principals arrived at the police station. Those involved were treated unusually when, rather than sitting out in the receiving area like common criminals, Florence, Harry and the wounded woman were spirited directly into the Chief's private office.

At the police station, the difference between the skills of those in the investigation and high class service staff was again apparent. As if ambivalent to the feelings of those involved, all the parties were grouped together in the one office. The service staff at the hotel had realized it was important to separate the parties.

As news that a shooting had occurred spread throughout the city, reporters were assigned to go to the police station to cover the breaking story. By the end of the first hour numerous reporters had descended upon police headquarters. Realizing the political implications, officers were placed around the doors to the interior rooms to keep the throng of reporters at bay. Since the principals in the case were sequestered comfortably away in the chief's office, reporters were unable to interview any of the parties. The reporters needed a story. Because the best they could do was see through the glass panel in the wall, the reporters wrote what they witnessed. The newspapers articles the first afternoon noted that the wife continued to cry hysterically, even after she was at the station.

Several reporters in their stories the next day commented on one incident. They noted how, in the anxiety of the situation, the wife appeared to ask that her husband give her a kiss. They noted what was believed to be a show of affection in the way she touched her husband's neck as he bent and presented her with the requested embrace. It was obvious to those covering the scene that the woman needed her husband for strength. Later, when Harry was seen crossing the room to consult with the wounded woman's physician, Flo called to him to return. Like an obedient child he returned to her side. Without Esek around, Florence had become the person whose role it was to dominate Harry.

As consumed as the reporters were by the emotion in the room, they were also intrigued by the dress of the woman who had fired the pistol. She wore a sky blue dress of the finest material, rings on each of her fingers, several of which had a diamond. To keep out the February cold she had on a sealskin sacque (a style of shawl). Over her stylish hat Florence Bussey had carefully draped a veil to prevent the reporters from seeing her too closely. Through the material of the veil the woman's white skin was striking enough that several reporters felt the need to report it to their readers. Despite her veil, those present noted that her beautiful face was contorted with a look of fear perceivable in her eyes.

The police chief, in an effort to alleviate the stress of having both the wounded woman and her assailant in the same confined space, moved Florence and Harry. He had the couple taken into the spacious empty courtroom, which was adjacent to the Chief's office. Special care was taken by the chief to assure that no reporters were allowed in the courtroom where the Busseys were sequestered. More important than separation for emotional reasons, the movement of the Busseys would give the chief the opportunity to question the wounded woman alone.

Upon arriving at the station, Judge Wheeler immediately assessed the situation. To be certain that discretion would be maintained, he took the Busseys into his private office. With this simple action he assured that they were out of harm's way and would be able to talk without being heard by the reporters.

When District Attorney Taylor arrived, he entered the Chief's office intent on interviewing the wounded woman. As she had in the hotel, the woman remained reticent to make any statements. Cajoled or intimidated, the woman finally broke and made a brief statement. The exact details of what she disclosed in that private meeting are still not certain even years later. Fortunately for the story, even in the 1880s there were unnamed sources that fed the press.

The wounded woman supposedly told of having received a note from an unnamed man. The note had asked that she meet with Mr. Bussey to discuss a problem that existed between the mystery man and Harry. As a favor, she had gone to the hotel to meet with Harry Bussey on behalf of the unnamed man. Ostensibly, the woman had gone to the Whitcomb House exclusively based on the note. There was no mention that Florence was supposed to be at the meeting. Pressed for details, she refused to give the name of the second man or even her own name. For clarification, the woman went on to insist that prior to the shooting there had been no problems between Florence and herself.

The wounded woman apparently included some details in the statement to the District Attorney. When she arrived at the suite the door was open. She entered the rooms to find that no one was present. As she turned to leave, Mrs. Bussey was standing in the doorway. From the wounded woman's report, it appears Mrs. Bussey had deliberately positioned her body to prevent her "guest" from being able to exit. In one report, Mrs. Bussey was holding the small gun as she initially blocked the doorway; in a second, she drew the gun during their ensuing conversation. In both reports she was blocking any means of egress.

Mrs. Bussey said to her soon to be victim, "So you are the woman who is running after my husband."

The woman responded, "No, I am not." Adding for effect, "I have no use for your husband."

Mrs. Bussey responded, "You lie." In one report, it was at this point in the confrontation that Florence drew a derringer from her handbag. In both reports, by this point the gun was pointed directly at the woman's forehead.

Despite facing the barrel of a gun, the woman was not intimidated. It would later come out that she was the daughter of a police officer, which may explain why she was so emotionally strong when it was required. She countered Florence's insult, "Be careful, madam, what you say. I think I am just as good as you are."

Mrs. Bussey replied with, "No you are not. If I should shoot you, I would be justified." Florence played her trump card saying, "I have very influential friends."

Accused of an amorous relationship with a married man and threatened with assault, somehow the alleged mistress remained calm in the presence of the jealous wife. The woman stared at Florence, thinking that there was no way that this spoiled rich woman would actually pull the trigger.

Florence Bussey responded to the brash stare by firing the pistol once into the woman's forehead. The gun was loaded with the black powder. The angle was steep; the powder old; the bullet small, so the ball had caught under the woman's skin. There was little visible damage except to the woman's skin. The two women were so close that when the gun was fired, some residue of the powder went into the victim's eyes. Going instantly into a state of shock, the wounded woman did experience a stinging sensation. It would turn out that the most serious part of the injury was the effect of the spent powder, a portion of which caused temporary burns to the victim's eyes.

Upon seeing what she had actually carried out, Florence Bussey responded in the form of all ladies of the Victorian Era. She fell to the floor screaming hysterically. According to the rules of society, Florence should have fainted, but that would have required truer emotions.

Despite the blood running from her forehead, the wounded woman remained bent over Florence's prostrate form trying to raise her from the carpet. Even with her own blood dripping onto the floor, the wounded woman continued to try to calm and reassure Florence.

The wounded woman tending to her assailant was the scene that the workers in the hotel found when they walked into the suite.

One must keep in mind that the wounded woman did not make a statement to the press the first day. Much of what was reported was either obtained from unnamed sources or was the reporter's speculation (possibly imagination).

The story continues to come out

Harry Bussey, however, did make a statement to the reporters the first day. His statement was limited because he was not present when the shooting occurred. By coming forward, Harry added much needed details to the otherwise convoluted tale unwinding at police headquarters. According to Harry's first report, several days prior to Florence and his excursion to Rochester, his wife had received a letter from a man named W. C. Thompkins. Although not in the Busseys' financial league, he was a reasonably successful manufacturer in Troy. Thompkins was the supervisor and proprietor of a knitting factory known as Brookside Mills. In the period just before the younger Bussey's move, Harry had been employed as the superintendent of the Standard Knitting Mill, a rival of the Brookside Mill. In the note, Thompkins pointed out to Florence that her husband had arranged to bring his lover with him in the move to Western New York. The letter in question went so far as to name the "other woman." Thompkins claimed she was one Rebecca Casey who, like the Busseys and Thompkins, was also from Troy. Unlike the Busseys and even Thompkins, Rebecca Casey did not move in the upper steps of Troy's social ladder.

It would be fair to characterize Thompkins as having ulterior motives when he sent the note to Florence. It is certain he was not being benevolent. It only took a day for reporters to learn that Thompkins had been rejected when he attempted to become Rebecca Casey's suitor. The fact that Rebecca was married to Edward Casey, a partner with his brother in a saloon in Troy, didn't seem to hamper Thompkins' desires or efforts. The speculation throughout the communities affected by this story was that Rebecca had chosen Harry over Thompkins. To those with any wisdom, the letter, therefore, was the act of a rejected lover.

It was soon ascertained that Rebecca Casey had worked at the Brookside Mill when Thompkins was the superintendent, but had later changed employers and had worked at Standard

Knitting Mill where Bussey was superintendent. By the time the story was printed it was understood that the Rebecca Casey noted in the letter was also known in the Troy area as Becky Lyons (start counting- she has two names so far).

According to Harry's first statement, when Florence read Thompkins' letter, she immediately confronted him with its contents. Harry attempted, without success, to assure her that there was no truth to the charges in the letter. Harry went on to explain to the reporters that his wife had a history of jealousy. In the case of the charges contained in the letter, Harry assured the reporters that he had tried for several days to reassure his wife but to no avail. Harry would be quoted as saying the "present trouble was, in a measure, the result of his own foolishness." He did not add detail to the comment.

Florence could be a pit bull when her jealousy button was pushed. Despite Harry's assurances that there was no need for concern, she would not let the matter drop. Harry, in an attempt to mitigate the situation, arranged to have Flo meet the infamous Rebecca Casey in Rochester. His stated intent in coming to Rochester was to put aside Florence's apprehensions brought on by the letter. The problem in the hotel was exacerbated by the fact that Florence did not know, and therefore would not recognize, Rebecca Casey.

The story took on a the colors of a full blown scandal when newspaper reports two days after the shooting stated that Rebecca Casey's husband was now suing the infamous woman for divorce.

Miss Irving joins the fray

The allegation running through both Rochester and Troy was that despite her protest, the wounded woman had finally been identified. She must be Rebecca Casey. In sharp contrast to Harry, the wounded woman continued to refuse to make any public statement. It was soon learned that the she had recently moved to Rochester with a friend named in the newspapers as Nellie Irving or Miss Irving (the use of the name Miss Irving was a sign of respect, implying the person was of some status or an elderly unmarried woman). Miss Nellie Irving was considered attractive and, like the wounded woman, she caught and held the attention of the reporters. Miss Irving immediately accepted the unsolicited role of serving as the wounded woman's public relations specialist. She made statements to the press and for a couple of days worked to get what she professed was the wounded woman's side of the story into the newspapers. It soon became obvious that there were reasons why it would not serve Miss Irving to have only the Bussey's story being reported. Nellie danced a fine step, since at the same time she was trying to get the wounded woman's side of the story into the newspapers; she was trying to keep her own story out.

Add a dash of Nash

Two days after the notorious shot in the Whitcomb House the story took a yet a second theatrical turn. Suddenly, a man named Charles Nash of Cohoes arrived in Rochester. Like Miss Irving, Nash wanted his story, at least as it related to Harry, in the newspapers. Nash's stated intent in coming to Rochester was to be sure that the Harry Bussey named in the accounts was the same man he knew from Troy (like there were two). What he accomplished was to add yet another account of Harry's behavior to the media fray that was developing.

Cohoes and Troy are separated by the Hudson River but the social differences between Charles Nash and Harry Bussey could never be bridged. Hearing reports of the shot, Nash said he boarded a westbound train to ensure the truth came out. Although most of the specifics were never published, Nash's revelations about the fast life that Harry Bussey led in Troy, added fuel to the blazing fire.

According to Nash, less than four months after the young Busseys had married, Harry had been named the correspondent in a divorce case in Troy. Nash went so far as to name the other couple as the Kennedys. In a time when divorce was uncommon, Nash maintained that Mr. Kennedy had been able to acquire a divorce claiming intimacy between Harry and Mrs. Kennedy. Nash went on to add that after hearing the report about her husband and Mrs. Kennedy, Flo had filed a similar claim against her husband; later, the two reconciled and her legal action was withdrawn. Nash assured the reporter that he had known Harry Bussey for some time, although, according to Nash, Bussey went by "Dick" in Troy. This is the only account where Bussey was called Dick. In all the others, including those from Troy newspapers, he was referred to as Harry.

Nash maintained that Harry had been "given" the position of Superintendent of a knitting mill in Troy. The implication was that this position was the result of his father's connections, not Harry's business capability.

Nash then went on to elaborate on his own family situation commenting that he and his young wife had "bright and encouraging" prospects. That was until she went to work in Harry's mill. Nash assured the one reporter that took the time to listen, how Mrs. Nash did not need to work. Nash even went so far as to say that her employment was "in violation of his wishes." It was the Victorian Era and one of the measures of a man's worth was whether or not his wife was employed outside the home. A working wife implied that the husband had insufficient income to support the family. Nash maintained that while his wife was working in the mill, Harry managed to steal her affections. Whether, the reason was Harry or not, Nash and his wife had separated shortly after she took the position in the mill.

The reporter took the time to wire a contemporary in Cohoes be sure of credibility of his source (Nash). It was learned that Nash was never the serene husband. Further, he had recently been fined $25 for molesting his own wife (this would have been almost a month's salary). When Nash was confronted about his own behavior, he felt that a great injustice had been done to him with the fine. He felt an even greater injustice that he had had to post a $1000 bond as assurance that he would never again molest his own wife. Nash, who had come to Rochester bent on exposing Harry, was indignant at the very presumption that a court could interfere in matters between a husband and wife.

Nash went on to explain that to rid himself of the woman to whom he no longer want to be married, he had offered her money to file for divorce against him. He maintained that she refused. Nash's wife told him it would please him too much to be free. Nash said he was going from Rochester to Connecticut to seek a divorce in that state on the charge desertion. He had, after all, offered his wife either reconciliation or a divorce and she would accept neither.

Nash was not one to leave quietly. He reminded the reporter that his purpose in coming to Rochester was to see if the Harry Bussey he had read about was the same as had been involved with his wife in Troy. Nash assured the reporter that he could give even more details about other relationships Harry Bussey had maintained with women while in Troy, but was sure that he had already established Harry's character to everyone involved.

Despite any feelings of grandeur Nash may have held by actually having his name appear in the newspapers, the only thing that he really added to the story was a little more detail. However, that changed when Nash reminded everyone that there was still uncertain the identity of the woman who had been shot. As a parting blast to Rochester, Nash added the prospect that the woman who had been shot was own wife, not Rebecca Casey.

Media Relations

The story of the shooting got very different coverage on the various days that it remained in the newspapers. At times Harry was supported in the newspapers, yet a day or two later another article in the same newspaper would condemn him and/or his lifestyle. One of the best examples of this inconsistency was in the series of articles that appeared in the *Troy Times*. In the early reports Harry's reputation was called into question. Later, a report was carried that held that the entire situation was the result of a scam gone wrong. The later story maintained that the woman who had been shot wanted to gain a settlement from the Bussey family's fortune. *The Troy Times* said that on several occasions women had attempted to "blacken" Harry's reputation by accusations of infidelity. Although never named, it appears from an article that would run later that the source of these revelations was Harry's father, Esek Bussey. In fairness, it would have been inconvenient for Harry to have outside relations while he lived in Troy. He and his wife resided with his father who was the arch-typical Victorian father set on watching his son's comings and goings. Harry's living arrangements did not make the accusations impossible, merely very difficult.

Divorce or aggravation

On January 16th, the day before Harry and Florence moved to Perry, a man appeared at the Bussey and McLeod Foundry attempting to serve legal papers on Esek. One reporter who followed up on this aspect of the story learned that the man was employed by Edward Casey's attorney. Edward was the husband of Rebecca Casey, the woman mentioned in the letter from Thompkins. The papers were copies of a legal complaint against Rebecca Casey charging that she and Harry had spent the night of January 9, 1884 together in hotel in New York City. This was the night that Harry had gone to the city to purchase equipment for the new mill in Perry. The legal papers that were served on Esek were inclusive of all the charges the husband was filing against his wife. Integrated in the complaint was an assertion that Rebecca had traveled overnight with another man on yet another occasion. There was little legitimate purpose in serving the senior Bussey except that he could testify that his son had gone out of town on the night in question. Serving the legal papers at the company office, however, provided embarrassment for the family, which, as subsequent events that day would show, was exactly what Edward seemed to have in mind.

After the process server left the foundry he went to the Bussey home to serve papers on Florence Bussey. Again, Florence could have added little to the evidence, but her well-documented fiery temper could serve as the catalyst for the truth to come out. Edward's real motivation, which was agitation, was apparent when it was learned that he also sought to have legal papers served on Mrs. Wilson, Florence's mother. Mrs. Wilson was still living in Chicago and would have no knowledge of the events of the night of January 9th.

After Esek was served he confronted his son. Harry quickly pointed out to his father that arrangements, such as those stated in the complaint, could not have happened. It seems that Esek and the man that was to be Harry's partner had spent the afternoon discussing the final terms of the merger of Standard Knitting of Troy and the manufacturing facility in Perry. Harry reminded his father that the trip to New York, which was to purchase new equipment, was a last minute decision based on the settlement. Harry went on to remind his father that the negotiations had gone on so long that he had less than half an hour to pack and get to the train. This timetable, according to Harry, left no time to make arrangements to meet this lady, Rebecca, or any one else for that matter, in New York City. Harry went on to remind his father that he (his father) had made the arrangements himself to pick Harry up at the train station after he had had to continue on to Providence. In Harry's defense it should be remembered that the telephone was still not a household appliance, so making any arrangements on short notice would have been difficult. Hearing his son's explanation, Esek was reassured that Harry was innocent, at least in this incident.

Esek makes a statement

In a prepared statement, Esek gave the family's official side of the story of what happened in Rochester. According to Esek, after Harry had moved to Perry he received a note from a fellow manufacturer in Troy. The man asked that Harry do him a favor and employ the woman known as Rebecca Casey. In the letter, which, if Esek's tale is to be believed, came two weeks before the shooting, the fellow manufacturer also asked that a second woman be hired. In his response, Harry agreed to hire both of women. As proof this was a favor to another person, Esek went on to tell how Harry had told his friend that he could not assure him that the women's jobs would be in or near each other in the mill in Perry.

Ida Brown

It was the day after the shooting that there was a probable identity of the woman who was shot. Her name was believed to be Ida Brown, the daughter of a former Saratoga County deputy sheriff. Raised in the resort city of Saratoga Springs, Ida's father suffered from consumption (TB). Over time his health had declined to a point that he was forced to retire. His disability occurred a few years before the incident in The Whitcomb House.

Brown had not stayed in Saratoga after he retired, choosing instead to move to Albany. He was joined in his move by his wife and some of their children. Brown lived less than a year after he retired to Albany. Following her father's death, Ida had not stayed with her family in Albany. Not poor, but in need of a steady income, Ida had taken employment in the mills of nearby Amsterdam.

Ida was a born beauty. If Ida was not aware of her unusual attractiveness while still living at home, she learned of her effects on men as soon as she moved out on her own. To some, especially those who are jealous or wish to blame the ills of the world on the good fortune of others, Ida was considered almost too beautiful for her own good. While living independently in Amsterdam, she would usually join in the Victorian entertainment of taking a stroll in the evening. On these walks she perfected the art of a being a coquette. It was easy to prove she was a flirt but there was little evidence of any behaviors beyond innocent flirting.

Try as hard as they could, reporters were unable to find a single source that would cast aspersions on Ida's character. Born poor enough to have to work in a mill, her limited funds were legitimately earned and not gifts. In all the reports Ida was consistently a woman of character. So why would she be shot?

Sometime in 1881 Ida relocated from Amsterdam to Troy where she took a job in a knitting mill. To those following this story in the newspapers, the circle now appeared to be closing. To those in the rumor business the answer was obvious; Ida had met Harry in one of the mills. But then again, everything is not as straightforward as it sometimes seems.

If this story does anything, it proves one more time that truth is stranger than fiction *and far more interesting*.

A week before the shooting Ida Brown had come to Rochester in the company of Nellie Irving. The two women were planning to open a women's fancy goods store (the Victoria Secret of it time). Women's undergarments were just developing into a publicly displayed specialty item. According to Nellie, she and Ida had obtained funds and were in Rochester looking for a storefront where they could sell items that would make women feel more attractive, even if the garments were not seen by others. So serious were the women about their business venture that it was learned that they had already arranged for space in the Miller Block on Monroe Avenue. It was reported that they had already received their first shipment which was being transported from the train station to the new store at the time of the shooting.

The other woman changes

Now that Ida's identity was reasonably confirmed, the newspaper accounts ignored further stories about Mrs. Nash and Rebecca Casey, choosing instead to portray the problem as between Florence and Ida, the two women who were in the room in the Whitcomb House. By the third day after the shooting it was believed that Mrs. Casey had never been Florence's intended target but served merely as an interesting distraction.

One newspaper went further suggesting that Florence had been jealous of Ida Brown from the time they both lived in Troy. It was widely reported that Florence's jealousy was so overwhelming that she had insisted on opening all of Harry's correspondences whether received at home or at his office. In this account, the jealousy was a major component of why the Busseys had sought to move from Troy to Western New York. There was suddenly a different perception of Florence. It was suggested that Florence had prevailed upon her father-in-law to set his son up in some out of the way hamlet?

Was Harry to be believed?

Harry's story was now, that in order to silence his wife's jealousy, he had agreed to have the other woman and his wife meet in a hotel in Rochester. Based on some of the facts that were coming out, Harry was suddenly being believed. Of course, as the story continued to break, readers shifted their belief from the other woman being Rebecca to the woman being Ida. This change happened despite the letter that had referenced Rebecca Casey by name.

It appeared that if Harry's idea had gone as planned when Florence and Ida met at the Whitcomb House, his wife would learn from Ida's "own lips" that there was no truth to the rumors and innuendos contained in the letter from Thompkins. What Harry did not know was that his wife had been carrying a 22-caliber derringer-style gun in her handbag for over a year. In a time before anything even vaguely resembling political correctness, the newspapers were universally opposed to women carrying guns. They used this incident to remind their readers that women could not be trusted with the responsibility of carrying a firearm. No one pointed out that men were much more accustomed to using guns on each other than women ever were.

Rumors fly

Several unsubstantiated stories started to emerge. One story held that Harry believed that the right woman might have been able to dissuaded Florence's jealousy. Another article suggested an interesting twist. In this article the allegation was that Harry had considered hiring another woman to pose as Ida. Other articles said that Ida was hired to portray the missing Mrs. Casey mentioned in the letter.

There was one serious flaw in all the speculation of a substitute. Ida was the wrong person to choose to dissuade a wife's jealousy. Any wife, especially Florence, would not be comfortable when she saw for herself Ida's natural beauty.

How the meeting came about

It was now understood that the actual arrangements for a meeting between the two women were easy. Harry had somehow learned that Ida had come to Rochester with Miss Irving to open a store. Knowing she was so close, Harry had contacted Ida to set up the meeting. No one took the time to question how Harry had learned that Ida was living in Rochester.

Nellie Irving reappears

In the days just after the shooting, the source of information about the wounded woman continued to be provided by Nellie Irving. The third day Nellie confirmed the reports from the previous day, acknowledging that Ida Brown was the woman who had been shot.

Nellie told the newspapers that the relationship that had made Florence jealous was not between Ida and Harry. Nellie said the problem was in fact between Harry and the Rebecca Casey, the woman whose name was in the letter from Thompkins. According to Nellie, Ida had somehow been convinced to accept money to portray Rebecca Casey in a meeting with Mrs. Bussey. Suddenly, the rumor that Ida was a hired double appeared true.

Nellie elaborated, saying Ida had come to the hotel with the intention of meeting with both Harry and Florence Bussey to assure Florence there was no relationship. When Ida got to the hotel she had gone to one of the parlors where she assumed she was to meet the Busseys. While waiting in the parlor, a porter came up to Ida giving her a note that asked her to come to Suite 19. The note was signed simply "H." Nellie said that Ida now believed that the note had been written by Florence, not Harry. This may have been the case, since Florence could in all probability have learned to sign Harry's name.

Nellie went on to say that Ida's only motive for agreeing to participate in the meeting with the Busseys was money. Nellie pointed out that Ida was poor. Because of her need for money Ida had decided that she might as well earn the money Bussey was offering, to fool his wife.

Probably as a reward for her being such an outstanding source, the same article went on to describe Nellie Irving in more detail than the earlier reports. She was portrayed as being nearly as attractive as Ida. More important was the much valued description of being a lady. One reporter depicted her as a "very pretty and a lady like young woman." Nellie was depicted as having had a passing acquaintance of Harry Bussey in Troy.

To keep her name clear of the shooting, Nellie was quick to point out that she cared no more for Harry than she did her handkerchief. Nellie indicated that she was a true friend and as such she intended to stick by Ida. This despite the implications of associating with a woman who was as notorious as Ida could have on Miss Irving's own reputation.

Before the meeting with the reporter was done, Nellie made one more attempt to clear her own name pointing out that she had never been on friendly terms with Harry and resented anyone who tried to cast aspersions on her reputation by implying that she had. She assured the people of Rochester that she intended to stay in the city, open her fancy goods store and prove her good name by living down the rumors that had started.

When confronted by newest revelations made by Nellie, Harry was reported to say simply that he "regretted the whole affair." Harry said that on the advice of others he had decided his best course was to just let the situation develop and not make any further statements. After saying he was going to be silent, Harry went on to express regret about the impact of the story on his family in Troy. Harry assured everyone that he was not guilty of any transgression with regard to Miss Ida Brown.

Harry, who moments before said he was going to remain silent, continued making two other telling remarks. He said that he had only met Nellie Irving and Miss Brown six weeks before in Troy. He made it clear that this meeting was on business (this of course led to a belief that Harry had been the source of funding for their store). Far more important, he reinforced yet again the knowledge that his wife was consumed by jealousy. He said that Florence had become very nervous lately. To alleviate some of his wife's anxiety he had agreed to the meeting in Rochester. So severe was Florence's fretfulness that Harry told reporters he did not think she had slept more than an hour a night for several nights before the incident. He tried to explain away the situation by saying his wife became quite insane and not responsible for her actions at the hotel. In the trials of the period, when an insanity plea was going to be entered, the defense always discussed eating habits and sleep patterns in the days before an incident. It appears, from his statements, that Harry was setting the stage for an insanity defense if necessary.

Even before Harry's assertions that Florence was jealous and nervous, the district attorney had asked a physician to check on Florence Bussey's mental condition. The prosecutor wanted to determine if the perception that was being presented, that Florence was not responsible, was in fact accurate. The implications of the district attorney's actions were to determine the probability of an insanity defense.

As Nellie had remarked that she was going to stand by Ida, Harry assured the community that he would stand by Florence.

Why were the women alone?

Unfortunately for everyone involved, Harry had gone to the hotel's office when Ida received the note in the parlor. Harry's absence meant that Florence was alone on the second floor when Ida arrived at the suite. It was never clear where Florence was when Ida first got to the room or why the door had been left open.

Trial?

As early as the first days following the shooting, the newspapers were reporting that they doubted that a trial would ever occur. The speculation abounded that the entire incident would be settled quietly out of court. It was projected, without being directly stated, that the Busseys' money had some benefits, and one of them would be solving this particular problem.

It was quite natural that Harry had little trouble raising the money that would be required to post bond. There was a serious problem, however, of getting Mrs. Bussey to the courtroom so the judge could order the bond. According to Harry and her doctor, Florence had barely slept since the shooting. Her stress continued and the doctors were unsure when she would be physically and emotionally able to return to the court.

Esek speaks out again

On the other side of the state, Esek Bussey released his second media statement. In that statement he seemed to support the concept presented by Nellie and Harry that the whole affair was one for money. Esek added that someone was deliberately trying to anger Florence. Esek maintained that on several occasions he had had to deal with agents for women who had tried to reach a settlement for supposed incidents involving Harry. These "designing women" made it a practice to say they were going to "blacken Harry's name" if they were not paid a remuneration. On each occasion Esek had learned that the women had manufactured the entire issue in an attempt to avail themselves of some of the Bussey fortune. Esek pulled no punches calling each of these assertions "blackmail."

Esek supported his claim by providing a letter that had been received by Florence when she was still living in Troy. This letter had come to the Bussey home at the same time as the papers which had the charges served by Edward Casey. The letter, which the handwriting indicated was written by a woman, said:

> The woman named in these proceedings [Rebecca Casey] is a woman that your husband has been furnishing with money for some time. She has frequently visited him in his office, and he promised to take her and another equally bad woman to Perry to work at the mill there for him. This trip to New York was merely a prelude to the future Perry business. They went to New York on the same train. Then met again in the evening and went to this assignation house together and made it their

headquarters during their stay. Your husband told friends in New York that he was stopping at the Sturtevant House, which was false as he had not been, or was ever known to any one connected with that hotel.

There is to corroborate these facts several parties besides the cab-driver that drove them to the ___ House Thursday night, the two cab-drivers that followed two colored servants in the house of prostitution, including the madam of the house, a Mrs. ___

"A Witness"

The two blanks were left out of the original newspaper account probably in an effort to avoid a suit for slander by the owners of the disorderly house in New York.

This letter had been received by Florence while Harry was at work. When Harry and his father arrived home Florence was ready for a fight. Esek described Florence as "much excited" saying she demanded to know the "truth in the matter." There, in front of his father, Harry accounted for his whereabouts the entire trip.

In his statement Esek went on to say Harry argued, "How could I do this? I did not see the woman before I left Troy on the day I went away." Harry had added, "I did not know I was going until a half-an hour before the train started." Harry was able to get his wife and father to see that, "It is a conspiracy to extort money from me and to cause trouble in the family." Harry went one step further. Unable to leave an argument not fully exposed, Harry made a statement that would come to bite him later. He added, "I would not know Mrs. Casey should I meet her in the street." This fight between the Busseys had occurred on January 17th, the day before the move.

According to Esek, Harry's explanation of what happened on the trip was sufficient for both he and Florence. Esek did go on to say that at the time Florence had declared to both men that evening that, "No woman would ever come between her and husband and take him from her."

To explain how Mrs. Casey came to be in Western New York, Esek provided a copy of the letter that Harry received from the manufacturer in Troy asking that he hire Mrs. Casey. This is the letter Esek had referred to in his first statement to the press. The letter differs from the explanations that had been circulating. In the written letter, the man does not request that Harry hire two women as Esek had said. In fact, the text indicates exactly the opposite.

> Friend Harry:
> If it is among the possibilities give Mrs. Casey employment. I do not think it will be long, as I can then place her elsewhere, but she will not come here now. It will be considered a personal favor, and if it ever should come my way I will return the compliment. Will be a favor to me if you say nothing of this letter. She knew I questioned you about the messenger.
> P. S. Should a girl named Ida Brown apply to you for work lookout for her. *She is no good.*

Based on Esek's information, interest in both Ida Brown and this Mrs. Casey intensified. It turns out that Ida had at least one sister. The sister that was found was married to M. S. Cummings, the clerk of the village of Saratoga Springs. When questioned about his sister-in-law, Cummings was surprised to hear she was in Rochester. The last time the family had heard from her she was living in Troy. Cummings went on to say that Ida had only been in Troy for two or three months. Ida's father had died less than a year before and she had moved from Amsterdam back to Albany to live in the respectable home with her mother. Until recently, Ida had commuted daily by train to her factory position in Troy.

Peace at last

The stories in the newspapers were all beginning to fit together like the pieces of a complex puzzle. Everyone, Esek, Nellie and Harry, were all saying that Florence was jealous to the point of insanity. With Florence bedridden from stress, her mental condition did seem to support their claims. Further, they all held that her jealousy was unwarranted. More important, all three representatives that were speaking to the newspapers alleged that Harry was a good man. Harry's care and warmth for Florence was most recently demonstrated in police headquarters where he had had been seen as gallantly calm and reassuring to his wife.

What Esek, Harry and Nellie were not saying was that

before the incident in the police station, Harry had tried to relieve his wife's stress by deceit. He had hired a woman (Ida) to pose as Mrs. Casey in an attempt at relieving the pressure on his family brought on by the letter from Thompkins. After days of having their names appear in the newspaper it looked like the story would probably finally end.

Wrong

The explanation for the events probably would have worked and peace would have followed if it were not for the exposure of one person's identity. On the fourth day it was learned that the woman known as Nellie Irving was, in fact, Rebecca Casey (name 3). The door to scandal, which had been slowly closing, was again thrown wide open.

Reporters learned that Rebecca Casey also had only one sister. Like Ida's sister, Rebecca's sister had married into a well-respected family in Troy.

An unnamed source came forward who tried to tie up some of the loose ends with respect to the parts of the story that occurred in Troy. That source placed Ida and Rebecca as coworkers at the Standard Knitting Mill (Harry's). According to this source, they were both there while Harry was the superintendent of the mill. The source said Ida was fired and Rebecca resigned in spite. The source was great at providing details, including the fact that the two women then went to live at a Mrs. Donaldson's on River Street in Troy. This would have been an interesting choice of residences, since Mrs. Donaldson's address is only a couple of buildings away from Casey Brothers Saloon. This is the business owned by Edward Casey, Rebecca's husband. Mrs. Donaldson was the agent for a corset company and both Rebecca and Ida had been known to work for her on occasion. The source went on to say that it was Harry's initial intention to bring Rebecca and Ida to work for him in Perry. After Edward Casey's agent served the divorce papers at the Bussey's foundry, Harry thought it wiser not to bring the two women so close to hearth and home. Instead, he had agreed to bring Rebecca to Rochester where she would open her own store but still be near enough to visit. (The person probably meant that Ida was fired from Thompkins Brookside Mill, since it would not have made sense for Rebecca to follow Harry if he had fired her.)

With all the news about his wife, it seemed important to one reporter to get Edward Casey's perception of the events that were unfolding. Edward said that he and Rebecca Lyons (Becky Lyons) were married for 8 1/2 years. They had only lived together for the first year and a half. It was then that he found out that his wife was unfaithful and had sent her packing. For seven years they had been apart and, according to Casey, he had recently filed for divorce. His decision was based on a report he had that his wife had been in Harry Bussey's company in New York City. Casey went on to say that Rebecca had been "kept by another well known mill owner for several years." (Thompkins?) He didn't say why he had not filed for divorce while she was a kept woman, but did express the depth of his feelings for her now adding, "I wish they would hang her." Casey was still convinced (perhaps hopeful) that the wounded woman was his wife.

The articles where the reporters were successful in pulling Edward Casey out of the woodwork also brought out Rebecca Casey in full force. The letter received by Florence had started sparks that had flickered, but with the comments by Edward, there were now full-fledged flames. The hostility among the various parties was burning at the reputation of everyone involved. The press of Rochester and Troy were, in fact, having a field day over what was being discovered. Not unlike today, the people of the Victorian Era like to see that wealth and good upbringing did not free people from shame and dishonor.

After the story broke that Nellie Irving, Becky Lyons and Rebecca Casey were the same person, it took Rebecca a day to get her side of the story out. When she was finally heard, the first thing she wanted understood was that she had never been in New York City with Harry. Rebecca's credibility had been seriously hampered by her use of other names and by her quote that Harry meant no more to her than her handkerchief, so why she expected anyone to believe her would be speculation.

Rebecca expressed her opinion to any member of the press corps who would take the time to listen to her, and some did just for the fun of the story. Rebecca went on the record that the entire set of events was the handiwork of W. C. Thompkins. She pointed out that she had made it a practice not to speak to Thompkins on "account of his vile reputation." This was interesting since in the same interview she claimed to have been a supervisor at Thompkins' mill. She also tried to clarify a part of Ida's employment history. According to Rebecca, Ida had never worked for Bussey. Ida had been employed by Thompkins in Troy. According to Rebecca, it was Thompkins that had fired Ida, not Bussey.

Rebecca pointed out that Tompkins was "crazy over" her (Rebecca). She told of how, in efforts to show his affection, he would do foolish things. She gave an example of how on one occasion he had jumped out of the third floor window in the American Hotel. Ever the modest one, Rebecca was quoted as saying, "He was so crazy in love with me that he was a fool and ought to have hanged himself." She went on to say she was surprised to find that Thompkins and her husband were suddenly friends, as they had been in fist fights the previous summer.

Rebecca attempted to explain away the impression that she had been kept by a businessman in Troy by pointing out that she had only taken money from Thompkins to pay for the cost of an attorney to get a divorce from her husband. Remember that it was her husband that had filed against her, so one would wonder where the money given by Thompkins went.

The Busseys' story

Although the name of the man who sent the letter to Harry asking that he employ Rebecca is not given, the Bussey family now had the situation figured out. Esek made sure that their vision of the events made it to the newspapers. To the Busseys, the entire mess was all the handiwork of W.C. Thompkins. His attentions toward Rebecca had been rejected. It was probably because he had made a play for Ida. When Ida told Rebecca of Thompkins' advances, he tried to demonstrate that his deeper feelings were for Rebecca, so he dismissed Ida. Instead of winning Rebecca back, both women left his mill and his embrace.

The Bussey family maintained that the two women then started scheming a way to get money and launched on a plan to blackmail Harry. Harry, after all, was married and had something to lose while Thompkins was not married. Thompkins might not like his name smeared but his reputation had little to lose. What they may not have realized is that everyone who commented in the newspapers did not feel that Harry had a particularly strong character. This was exemplified by Rebecca's characterization: "He (Thompkins) had said that he would fix Bussey and thinks Bussey has no nerve." She went on to say, "I guess he is right."

There are two possibilities as to who wrote the letter to Florence. Either it was Tompkins who wanted to get even with Harry, or it was arranged by the two women as blackmail. In either event, it was probably not the result of a deep emotional relation between Harry and Rebecca. Poor Ida, the wounded woman, was just a pawn in a game far more complicated than she had assumed.

Where did Rebecca get the money to start a fancy goods store? Rebecca was quoted in several newspapers as saying that, "Mr. Bussey never promised nor did he ever set me up in business." She went on to say that she, "had the wherewith all to go into business for herself independent of anyone." In all probability, it was the money that Thompkins had given her to get a divorce.

Slow to recover

Florence was unable to appear in court the on the fourth day to respond to the possible charges to be filed against her. The district attorney and an attorney for Bussey met and agreed to postpone any hearing on the issue for two weeks. The official reason for the postponement was the physical condition of the two women involved.

Time to get out of town

It was time for everyone to leave Rochester and let the rumor pot cool. The day after Florence was too ill to appear in police court, it was discovered that Ida and Rebecca had left their hotel. The hotel where they were staying said they kept the rooms and had traveled with only a small valise. The two women were reportedly seen in New York City. In case Harry might think that Ida was going to disappear quietly, the newspaper pointed out that she had retained an attorney to help the district attorney in his investigation.

The Busseys also left town. The same day Rebecca and Ida went to New York, Harry took a train to LeRoy. From there he connected with a train to Perry. Officially, he needed to get back to managing his mill. Florence Bussey's emotional condition was described as deplorable. At a hearing two weeks after the shooting, her bail was set at $4,000, which was put up without delay by an agent for the Bussey family. Mrs. Bussey followed her husband to Perry a day later. It was the opinion of the doctors that Florence was suffering from acute mania and was temporarily insane at the time the shot was fired.

Esek came out one more time for Harry saying that the two women had been following his son for several weeks in an attempt to extort money from him.

The press now took the position that the true motive for angering Mrs. Bussey was to blackmail Harry. The press could never really establish whether Ida was a willing participant in the blackmail or a relatively innocent friend who was tricked into her role.

And then

This story, like many true crime tales from the Victorian Era, did not have a true ending. Instead, it faded into some obscure abyss waiting for discovery. In just days the space it had occupied in the newspapers was replaced by some other tale that held the area's attention again for a brief moment. Even out of the headlines, those involved in the Whitcomb House shooting had lives that continued.

The most famous character in this cast would turn out to be Harry Bussey. Harry was head of the mill in Perry for less than two years. During that time, the mill increased in capacity but did not realize a profit. Harry sold his interest in the mill and bought a tavern and hotel in the center of the Village of Perry. Harry maintained the Tavern for over twenty years. Harry and his wife built a large Victorian home on the way into the village. Today, the house is a halfway house for troubled adolescents (an interesting choice based on Harry's problems).

More interesting, Harry went on to have a political career. One of the first steps was his election as President of the Village of Perry (this position was the equivalent to Mayor today). His political career did not end at the local level. Shortly after the turn of the century, Harry was elected New York State Senator from his district. In this capacity he even made *The New York Times* for his vote to impeach Governor Sulzar.

In some ways this is the case of missing people. The Busseys never had children and interestingly, Florence moved back to Troy where she died while quite young. Harry remarried and had a daughter. Harry stayed on in Perry until about the time that Esek Bussey died in 1916. Harry then moved somewhere, but not back to Troy.

The only one who appears to have any degree of innocence was Ida Brown. After two weeks, Ida Brown dropped from the roles. The fate of this beauty could not be found.

Rebecca Casey, like Ida, was not found but one can be assured she continued to change names more often than others change clothes.

It is intriguing that this group of players had lives that, for one week, charged the curiosity of thousands, yet then faded into obscurity.

Hattie Munckton

"Somethin's burned me."

Along the eastern end of the Mohawk River, there are few meteorological phenomenon more destructive than an August thunderstorm. There is something about the way the river valley is surrounded by the Catskills, Berkshire, Green and Adirondack Mountains and the way the heat and humidity build during the summer days that work together to prevent the moist air from escaping. The mixture of topography and humidity creates an atmosphere ripe for violent storms. These storms have a fondness for appearing in the late afternoon or in the overnight hours.

His Story

With thunder rumbling outside, it was only natural that James Munckton would ascribe the loud boom that wakened him in the overnight hours of August 30/31, 1905 to the storm. The sound of the pounding rain on the windowsill reinforced his first impression. Opening his eyes, there was just enough light for Munckton to realize that his humble bedroom was smoky and his bedding was actually on fire. During those groggy moments that follow his arousal from a deep sleep, Munckton was sure that lightning had come in through the open window and struck his bed.

It was not until he actually got out of bed to extinguish the flames in the bedding that Munckton acknowledged that he had a serious wound. When the fire was out Munckton allowed himself to groan from the pain of his wound.

It was either the sound of his father's loud moaning or the boom that preceded it that awoke Munckton's thirteen year old son, George. George slept in a room at the other end of the small house. In the darkness of his room, the boy looked at the opposite side of the bed and noticed that his mother was missing. [The mother and son slept in the same bed in a room off from the living room while Munckton slept alone in a room off the kitchen.] With the sounds of groans continuing, George got out of bed and started through the house seeking the source.

One of the first things George noticed was that all the doors in the small home were closed. It was the family's practice to leave the interior doors open. Open doors in the hot summer allowed whatever breeze there was to cool the house. In the winter the doors were open so the rooms could be heated by a single woodstove.

When George opened the door between the living room and the kitchen he heard his mother, Hattie, call out, "Is that you George?"

He responded in the colloquial, "Yes, Ma."

The heavy clouds and the dark, moonless night had made the room so dark that George's mother could not be certain that the form she saw was her own son. His mother directed George to "Light a match." Following his mother's instructions George went to where the family kept their matches. He took one from the container, and lit the wooden stick in an effort gain enough light to cut through the blackness that permeated the chamber. As he lit the match, George could still hear his father's moans coming from the room off the kitchen. When George and his mother entered Munckton's room they only had the limited radiance of the match. Still George could make out the outline of his father's form standing near the room's window.

Now that there was light in his bedroom, Munckton looked down and examined his wound. From the outline of the blood he could see that the injury started below his heart with pain extending into his abdomen. The gravity of the injury was fixed in the minds of the three present when they saw the substantial amount of blood that had been lost.

When Munckton raised his gaze from the wound to his son's face, he told George that he had been "struck by lightning." Pausing for a moment, he continued, "Somethin's burned me." As George and his mother's eyes were fixed on the excessive blood, Munckton decided that it was not lightning saying, "I've been stabbed." By this time, Munckton was loosening his clothing, trying to see the extent of his injury. [The family slept in their clothes.]

After Munckton had seen the extent of his wound, Hattie put her arms around her husband's neck and said, "I wish I knew who did this."

Munckton's answer was direct and accusatory, "Hattie, you know who did it. You know you haven't been treatin' me right for some time."

Help

Finally grasping the seriousness of the wound, the couple sent George to get a neighbor call for help [they did not have a phone of their own]. Living in rural southern Saratoga County, George had few options of which house to run for help. He elected to sprint to the home of F. W. Grabo, one of his nearest neighbors. It would turn out that this was not the first time that Grabo had been called to intercede at the Munckton's home.

When Grabo came to the door, George told him that his father had been stabbed and needed help. Grabo dressed and rushed to the family's home where he found Munckton laying back in the bed, suffering from his wound. Examining Munckton, Grabo knew that the injuries were too serious for him to be of much assistance. Grabo rushed back home where he used his relatively new telephone to call Dr. Strang of Vischer Ferry.

Within minutes of arriving at the Munckton's house Dr. Strang began treating the injury as if it were the result of a gun shot, not lightning or a stabbing. Dr. Strang probed the wound, searching for the spent bullet. Unable to find the metal, Dr. Strang determined that his patient was injured far too seriously to be treated at home. In order to provide what emergency help he could, Strang stayed with Munckton but instructed Grabo to go home and get a wagon to take the wounded man to the Cohoes Hospital. Grabo took George with him to hitch the horse, leaving Strang alone with Hattie and Munckton. Strang took the opportunity to ask questions about what had occurred. Strang was told by both the husband and wife that Munckton had been struck by lightning. Despite the fact that the doctor stated his belief that it was not lightning, the couple would not bend in their tale.

In the black early morning hours, it was a dangerous six mile night drive over muddy rural roads to get to the Cohoes Hospital. Grabo drove the horse at speeds well beyond prudent, pushing aside his own safety; doing as was expected of a leading individual in the area. On the precarious trip, Mrs. Munckton sat in the back of the wagon comforting her husband. There was only a limited conversation between the couple; however, Grabo did overhear Mrs. Munckton say, "It is so queer, Jim, that a year ago you took me down and now I'm taking you down." It was a reference to another emergency trip to the hospital in Cohoes.

Upon their arrival at the hospital, Munckton was seen by Dr. Warren, the house physician. Both the Muncktons told Dr. Warren the story that the injury was the result of a lightning strike. Immediately upon examining the wound, Dr. Warren tried probing the wound in searching for the projectile. Unable to locate the bullet, Dr. Warren determined that surgery was necessary. He had a member of the staff summon Dr. Mitchell, chief of surgery, to assist. While awaiting Mitchell, Warren asked Munckton what had happened. James Munckton retold the story about being struck by lightening. Dr. Warren assured Munckton that the wound was not the result of lightning, suggesting as an alternative that the wounds were the result of a gun shot. Despite the doctor's insistence, Munckton would not deviate from his lightning story.

Treatment

Damage from a shotgun blast at short range can be massive. At 10:00 in the morning, Dr. Mitchell and Dr. Warren were operating on Munckton. Shortly after they opened his abdomen, the doctors found that his wound was more serious than they had anticipated. Although the entry wound was near the chest, Munckton's injuries were primarily in the lower abdomen, which had been literally shredded by birdshot. Based on the damage to the internal organs the two doctors made a difficult prognosis. They surmised that, based on the extent and location of the injuries, there was no way to save Munckton's life; the best they could do was to make his death as painless as possible. In only a few hours, the doctors' diagnosis would prove to be correct.

The rumors begin

Out of surgery and back in his hospital room, Munckton continued to fail. Sitting at his bedside with the family gathered in support, Hattie heard her mother-in-law and father-in-law talking. Hattie leaned over her husband and said, "For God's sake, get well for my sake. They think I did it." Her request went unheeded as Hattie's words were spoken only moments before Munckton expired.

James Munckton died at 4:30 in the afternoon surrounded by his wife, son and other members of the Munckton family.

The Media

After Munckton arrived at the hospital and told his story for the first time, Dr. Warren was skeptical and instructed one of the staff to contact the police. Even though the incident did not happen within their jurisdiction, the Cohoes police took two actions. They requested that Grabo come down for questioning, and they notified the Saratoga County Sheriff of the possibility of a suspicious shooting in his jurisdiction.

The newspapers the day following Munckton's death pointed out that no gun had been found and summarized the incident saying it was understood that the entire affair was "shrouded in mystery." The early newspaper reports generally stated that the family had resided together in reasonable harmony. One Troy paper went so far as to say of Munckton that "(he) was one of the best regarded residents of the section in which he lived."

By the second day the newspaper reports continued to comment on Munckton as a successful farmer but alluded to some disharmony in the home. The source of the conflict was suggested to be jealousy on the part of Munckton. Unnamed sources implied that there could be justification for Munckton's concerns of his wife's infidelity.

As is often the case, the first reports and the facts that came out in the months that followed were dramatically different.

The investigation begins

Since in 1905, both Clifton Park and Vischer Ferry were too rural to have their own police station. Two officers from Mechanicville were assigned to investigate the case. The officers were Deputy Hubbs and Detective Andrus, both of the Saratoga County Sheriff's office.

Even as Munckton was undergoing surgery, the police commenced their investigation of the shooting. The two officers took George to the Muncktons' house where they were greeted by a very loud dog. It was obvious the dog did not take to strangers. The dog was so excited that he could only be calmed by George. Naturally, the officers asked if the dog had barked during the night of the shooting. George responded that the dog had been still; reminding the officers that he was awakened by his father's groans, not the barking of the dog.

Walking around the house, the officers found that there were no footprints attributable to an intruder. There was, however, an axe found outside Munckton's bedroom window. There was no sign of a gun during a cursory search of the house, grounds and outbuildings. It would be another day before the gun was found hidden in a closet and the expired shell casing was found lodged behind a stair.

As part of the investigation the officers questioned the neighbors. The neighbors assured the officers that the Munckton's dog was quiet on the night in question. The investigation took its first twist when the people in the area told of some serious disagreements within the Munckton's home. Those interviewed told how some of the disputes were so serious that they required the intervention of those who lived in the neighborhood. According to several people, one of the worst fights had occurred the previous July. It seems that in the early evening, several neighbors heard two women screaming "murder." Neighbors who had rushed to the Munckton house reported they found Hattie locked in the cellar with her blouse torn at the waste. They found James Munckton in the kitchen with his shirt torn.

The suspect

In cases where there is a suspicious death, the spouse is always a person of interest. With only young George and his mother reported to be in the house at the time of the shooting and no unexplained tracks outside, Hattie was naturally the primary suspect. While the family was still at the hospital, several people, including the coroner, asked Hattie about the character of the family's relationship. In each case she assured whoever questioned her that things were the "happiest of sorts." When she was questioned by those at the hospital about the altercation that happened the previous July, Hattie brushed it off saying, "It amounted to little."

After being at the house, interviewing the neighbors and hearing what the wife had said to people during the day, both officers surmised that Hattie Munckton had to be the person who pulled the trigger. Their theory made sense. By Hattie's own account she was in the house at the time of the shooting (opportunity). During questioning, George told the police that the same evening, his parents had quarreled at dinner (possible motive). The dog had been silent, indicating that whoever fired the shot was familiar. From the officers' point of view it appeared that one person had both motive and access. She also lacked any legitimate alibi. The case against Hattie was further supported by the fact that she and Munckton held to the ridiculous story that he was hit by lightning. They refused to modify their story even when the doctors had said lightning was not the cause.

Based on the information they had gathered, the officers decided to confront Hattie. Naturally, they asked Hattie about the incident in July. She explained that it was an isolated occurrence, going on to add that she and her husband had always had a good relationship. This statement was made less than five hours after the death of her husband. Readers should keep in mind that in 1905, people actively practiced the precept of not speaking ill of the dead.

It was a time when police officers felt that to be effective they had to appear tough. The officers maintained this decorum when they bragged to the press that in order to obtain a quick confession, they had put Hattie through "the third degree." As the interrogation went on, more and more of the story began to emerge.

As early as the late Victorian Era, the strategy of good cop, bad cop was already in practice. Deciding to cut to the chase, one of the officers, Detective Andrus (bad cop), bluffed saying that they had enough evidence to send her to the electric chair. The other, Deputy Hubbs (good cop), suggested that if she confessed she might be able to get the charges reduced second degree murder. In that case she would have to serve a very long sentence but would avoid the electric chair. It was a bluff because at the time the officers had not located the weapon or an eye witness to the shooting.

Faced with a difficult choice, Hattie's answer was all the officers had hoped for, "Yes, I did shoot him. I would rather take the electric chair or go to prison for life than to live the life of hell and torture I have lived."

While he wrote up her confession, Officer Andrus allowed Hattie's sister, Mrs. Morehead, to give the "suspect" a drink of brandy. Given a tumbler, she drank the contents straight down. The statement read in part that she; "... *took the gun and fired at his form in the bed. Shot him because life had been a burden to me; he pounded me and struck me, and I often thought he was crazy the way he used me.*"

During the interrogation, Hattie told the officers that she had hidden the shotgun in a closet and that they could find the spent shell casing hidden in one of the stairs. She had hidden these things during the time George had gone to get Grabo. She had also thrown the axe out Munckton's window; however, the officers did not feel this was important enough to consider.

From the point of view of the police officers, the case was resolved. They had a body, a cause of death, the location of the weapon, and a self-confessed murderer. With no local jail set up to handle a woman inmate, Hattie was taken to a hotel in Waterford for the night. The next morning, in front of a justice of the peace in Mechanicville, Mrs. Hattie Munckton was arraigned on the charge of murder. She was remanded to the Saratoga County jail without bail to await her trial.

What the police did not have, however, was a case that could be considered a certain conviction. Because she had been given alcohol and did not have an attorney present when she confessed, there was a very real question as to whether Hattie's

114

written confession would stand up to a challenge in court. Even more important, in rushing for a resolution the officers had not heard the entire story.

All is not as it seems

Despite the quote in the newspaper, Munckton was not one of the most respected men in his section. He may have been a hard worker but he was not someone who dealt fairly with his family. As time progressed, it turned out that there were people who had witnessed examples of his displays of physical violence. These neighbors and family members told of multiple incidents between the couple, not just the one in July. There were also people who would come forward who had seen the bruises that resulted from an attack of the husband upon his wife. So serious had been the beatings that on at least one occasion Hattie had to be taken to the hospital for treatment of a broken jaw.

There were even people who had witnessed physical troubles with the son. In George's own words he "got a likin' 'bout every day" from his father.

When asked if his father ever hit his mother, George responded, "Not of'en, only 'bout once a week." We all have our own limits on what is acceptable but this thirteen year-old had witnessed so much that he was unable to understand what was normal.

Commentary

Rarely is there just one conflict between a couple that results in one of their deaths. It is far more common for there to be a history of issues building into problems and, in the cases that result in criminal actions, the problems have build into crises. Once one crises turns to violence, each subsequent issue escalates into physical altercations more quickly. This was the pattern in the Munckton family.

The Muncktons

George Munckton was 36 years old. His wife was slightly younger at 33; however, seeing her tiny, weathered appearance, one would have guessed she was older (most reporters assumed upon seeing her that she was at least 40). Married for 16 years, the couple had only the one child, George. At the time of the shooting, they lived on a rented property known as the Warren Farm, two miles north of Vischer Ferry, in the town of Clifton Park.

Both husband and wife had extended family in the area. James Munckton's father lived in place called Clute's Dry Dock, a hamlet on the Erie Canal near Crescent. He had a brother who lived and worked in Cohoes. Hattie's brother lived in Amsterdam and her mother, who was nearly blind, and a sister lived Schenectady. She had another sister who lived in Cohoes.

Both families had had problems with the law in the past and courtrooms were not unfamiliar venues. According to some of the testimony, Munckton said that his father and uncle had been in jail, adding, "I'll never go." Hattie's father had recently married; an act that had caused him problems with the law. It seems that when he married for the second time he had forgotten to divorce Hattie's mother. He would be convicted of bigamy while Hattie was in jail awaiting her own trial.

Over the course of their marriage, the Muncktons had lived in a variety of places, but almost always as tenant farmers. Although not living in poverty, the Muncktons usually eked out a living which allowed for few pleasures. They would not be considered middle class. The Muncktons grew produce, which was sold at various markets. Additionally, the family had a small dairy and kept chickens which they used for both meat and eggs. Like many farmers, Munckton supplemented his income by occasionally working at odd jobs.

Munckton was helped in his 'pursuit of happiness' by having his wife who was often employed as a day worker. Very early in the investigation it was learned that Munckton commonly hired Hattie out to work in the fields or to help split and stack firewood – the types of work that, at the time, was considered "men's work." Like many husbands at this period, Munckton would take Hattie's meager earnings when she got home. Although it was only in the last few years, James Munckton had started hiring out George to do farm work like he had Hattie.

It was not just learning that he was taking his wife's earnings that started Munckton's downfall as a "respected man in his section," it was the family's eating pattern and his propensity toward violence. For unexplained reasons the family often lacked sufficient food for three people. This may seem like a strange problem for people who earned a living from farming, especially when the farm had produce, poultry and a dairy. However, if one sells all he grows instead of putting some aside for the winter, he can run out. Whenever there was not enough food for everyone, James ate as much as he wanted first, then he allowed his wife and young son to eat.

A history of abuse

It would be difficult to place an exact date on when the violence in the Munckton household began. There were stories with exact dates given which occurred as long as four years before the shooting. In all likelihood there were probably incidents that went back even further. The record shows that there were several violent episodes that happened the summer prior to the shooting. The stories may be biased because they were primarily told by Hattie's family; however, there is no evidence that the stories were ever rebutted by the neighbors or by members of the Munckton family so they stand as the only official account.

On the wagon ride the night of the shooting, Hattie had reminded her husband that it was "queer" that she was taking him to the hospital when just a year before he had taken her to the same hospital. It was on that occasion that Hattie had had a broken jaw. When asked what caused his mother's injury, George responded without reservation, "Pa's fist." It seems that on the day of the jaw breaking incident, Hattie had had some unexpected company and had not finished the field work Munckton had assigned. When he realized she had not completed her assigned work, Munckton threw a cup of hot tea at her and said, "You are a lazy bitch," as he hit her with his fist.

There were a series of incidents that were discovered that all focused on Hattie's failure to finish her assigned work. On each occasion Munckton punished her with a thrashing.

There was one other incident that happened before the summer of 1905 that provides some indication of the extent of Munckton's behaviors, including his jealousy. According to Hattie, and not disputed when the story became known, one evening Munckton invited some men who worked at a local sandbank over to play cards. The group drank and played for some time. When the men left, Munckton accused Hattie of inviting the men into the house; the implication being that she intended to be more personal with one or more of the men. Munckton refused to hear Hattie's reminders that it was he who had invited the men inside. In anger Munckton took Hattie out into the woodshed and tied her to a post. Despite her calls for mercy, Munckton repeated over and over "they came to see you."

As she was being tied Hattie kept saying, "Oh dear, don't pound me. It wasn't my fault they came here." Her pleas fell on deaf ears as Munckton started beating her on the back repeatedly with a club.

Luckily the screams Hattie emitted were heard and several men in the neighborhood came to her rescue. The men grabbed Munckton, telling him they were going to have him arrested. In a behavior too typical of women living in this kind of relationship Hattie begged the men, "Now boys don't take him away, he's my husband and I don't want him arrested." Foolishly the men did as Hattie asked and released Munckton. When the men were leaving she called to them, "Don't let no one know what you saw here tonight."

Because of the number of people involved, the incident on July 9th had caused a lot of discussion in the neighborhood. All that day, Hattie and her sister had been out "berrying" on their father's farm. When they got home James was upset saying, "You earned eighty cents and twenty-five dollars worth of potatoes were ruined because you didn't put Paris Green on 'em." [Paris Greens was used as an insecticide. Because it is a poison the state made the use of Paris Greens illegal in 1906.]

Hattie knew there was no dealing with her husband when he was in this kind of mood so she and her sister went into the cellar to churn some butter. Munckton was not in a disposition to be ignored. He followed the two women into the cellar where he grabbed a broom stick and started beating on Hattie. In the fight that ensued, Hattie kept screaming and tried to get away. Her sister came to her defense trying to grab the arm that held the broom stick. When Munckton had Hattie by the throat, he called out, "I'm gunna murder you. I'll get the gun and murder the whole lot of you" [referring to his sister-in-law and George]. To hold his wife while he beat her, Munckton grabbed at the material of her blouse at the level of her waist. The material tore to shreds as Hattie escaped from his grasp. Finally free, Hattie and her sister ran outside screaming "Murder." Their combined screams aroused several of the neighbors.

Before the neighbors could get to the house the two women saw Munckton leave the cellar and go in to the kitchen. For safety they ran back into the cellar where they barricaded the door. Grabo and other neighbors had heard the commotion and came over to investigate. They found Munckton standing in the kitchen and realized Hattie was in the cellar. It took a while but the neighbors were able to convince Hattie to come out but when she emerged they could see her ripped blouse and other marks. Grabo told them that "such goings on were not right on a Sunday." In front of the neighbors, the couple shook hands assuring everyone the episode was over.

The incident may have been over as far as the neighbors were concerned; however, not for the Muncktons. That same night Hattie and her sister were so scared that they took Munckton's shotgun, his sword and George's rifle and placed them under the mattress of the bed. Hattie, her sister and George then nailed all the windows and bolted the doors and put nails in the jam to be sure Munckton could not enter. That night the three slept together in one bed in fear that Munckton would try to fulfill his threat.

It only took days for the next situation to erupt. On July 14th, there was another incident. Again the catalyst appears to be Munckton's belief that Hattie had not worked hard enough picking berries. This time the fight was in the kitchen and Munckton grabbed the butcher knife and threw it at Hattie's head. She snapped her head back in time and the knife struck the kitchen wall. Munckton continued his rage calling out, "You dirty lazy slutton. You're running all about town like a spotted dog." It is worthy of note that there are no statements, by anyone other than Munckton, that Hattie had been anything but faithful. In fairness to Munckton, Hattie is not described as the type of person a man would brag about having a relationship with.

There was at least one other incident that summer which was corroborated by a second party. In early August, Munckton came home and found his wife and son working the grinder sharpening some farm implements. Something in their behavior bothered Munckton and he said, "Why don't you turn the grindstone faster?" whereupon he picked up a blacksmith's hammer that was lying nearby and threw it at the members of his family saying, "I'll brain you." The hammer narrowly missed each of their heads. Walking away Munckton said, "I'll have your blood before fall," continuing his threat with, "I'll dance in your blood."

The injuries that Hattie received were so frequent that she started giving them names. A "Jim's size nine" was a bruise resulting from having been kicked. If he punched her, the bruise was referred to as a "pound."

August 30th - The day of the shooting

That morning, as Munckton and his son loaded the family's wagon with vegetables, it did not appear that the day would be in any way special. Father and son took the load of produce to a market in Schenectady. It was afternoon when they returned. Munckton left George at the house and drove to his father's house on the canal. Between six and seven in the evening Munckton returned to his own home.

Hattie was not in the house when Munckton arrived. She had not returned from working all day, cutting corn at a neighboring farm. When Hattie finally got home, a short time after her husband he greeted her with, "It's a wonder you know enough to come home to supper." He went on to belittle her adding, "Beats hell why you never have supper ready." In her own defense Hattie reminded Munckton that she had worked all day. Their exchange of hostile words continued throughout the preparation and eating of dinner.

Hattie was exhausted from working in the fields all day and knew there was no dealing with her husband when he was in such a mood. About 9:30 p.m., Hattie retired to her bed leaving Munckton to read his book alone. Before leaving the kitchen she gave her husband a kiss. It was a ritual the two had followed every night for the sixteen years of their marriage. No matter what the issues of the day, it was their practice to kiss before going to their separate beds.

At eleven, Munckton went into Hattie's and George's room and woke up his wife. He motioned for her to follow him. The obedient submissive that she was, she accompanied him to his room. According to Hattie, they were in his room for about fifteen minutes. It was long enough for him to hold her down and sodomize her. For Hattie it was the last straw. She told her husband, "Jim Munckton, tomorrow I'm going to swear out a warrant. I will have you arrested."

His response was predictable. "You shall never have me arrested." Going on he added, "You will never even live till morning. I'll blow your head off."

Fearing more violence, Hattie fled for the sanctuary of George's and her room. As she escaped she had the presence of mind to take the shotgun with her.

It was not long before she could hear noises coming from the kitchen. She called out, "Jim Munckton, what are you doing?" There was no answer. Eventually she heard the sounds of him going back to his own room. Fearing he had taken a knife or some other weapon, Hattie followed the sounds down to her husband's room.

As she was lighting a lamp she heard the sound of heavy metal dropping to the floor. When the room was lit she could see an axe lying at her husband's feet. Her eyes asked the question even before her lips moved. Munckton made his intentions clear. "I'm going to brain you and that brat!" The two argued, each threatening the other. Returning to the issue of having him arrested Munckton remarked, "My father and my uncle served time in jail but I never will."

With a coldness that would scare anyone, Munckton began sharpening the butcher knife with a wet stone. He looked up at his wife saying, "I'm going to cut your throat this minute."

Munckton reached out quickly grabbed Hattie and threw her on the floor. He then attempted to grab her by the throat with one hand. With the other hand, he tried to reach for the butcher knife to cut her throat. She was strong enough to knock the knife out of his reach. He released his hand from her neck saying, "Get out, I will kill you before morning."

Hattie fled to her room. When she was gone Munckton blew out the lamp and lay down on his bed.

Back in her room Hattie tried the windows. They were still

nailed shut from the incident on July 9th. She loaded the shotgun and sat on the side of the bed. Again she heard Munckton in the kitchen. Suddenly the noise in the kitchen ceased.

She waited a few minutes, then went back to Munckton's bedroom door. As she was opening his door, she bumped a chair Munckton had placed next to the door so she could not sneak in. When Munckton heard the noise he called out from his bed, "Damn you. I've got you at last."

She raised the shotgun to waist level and fired. As she fled out the door, Hattie dropped the gun. Munckton called out to his fleeing wife, "You've got me but I am going to brain you and the brat."

Hattie would later say she had not meant to kill her husband and that she was shooting at his feet. The truth of that statement is something that will never be known; however, the angles involved (her standing and him lying down) would explain how the wound went down from the chest to the abdomen.

A joint story

While George was on his way to get their neighbor, Grabo, Hattie and James talked quickly about the events of the day and evening. They were both in legal trouble. At the very least James could be charged with assault; possibly sexual assault [the laws governing behavior between a husband and wife were very different than now] and perhaps even attempted murder. On this one occasion, Hattie had gone one step further than her husband. She had actually shot Munckton. Hattie could be charged with attempted murder. In the brief time they had, the two agreed that she would not talk about the incidents during the day and night and that he would hold to a story that he was hit by lightning. For a day, each would keep their word.

In the few minutes she had, Hattie set about shielding them both. To protect her husband, Hattie threw the axe out the window. To protect herself she hid the shotgun in the closet and the shell casing behind a stair.

***

With Hattie in jail and Munckton dead, someone had to be assigned custody of George. It was decided by Judge Nash Rockwood that the paternal grandparents would have temporary custody. Relatively quickly, the judge would change his mind and have George placed in a state operated juvenal center in rural Westchester County. To an experienced observer this was the first indication that there may be more to the story of the family than had been explained.

While Hattie was in jail awaiting her trial, the only way for Hattie to keep clean was to use the jail's gang showers. In effect, she was forced to be nude in front of other women. When some of the other female prisoners were released, they started telling of the serious bruises they had witnessed on Hattie's body. According to these ex-prisoners, when Hattie entered the jail, she had black and blue marks all over her body and there were even some minor lacerations.

Trial

It was only three months between the shooting and the trial. The prosecutor was McKnight who was the assistant in the trial of the Nolan sisters. The judge in the trial was Nash Rockwood of Saratoga Springs. At the time of the trial Rockwood was going through a divorce himself. According to reports his wife, who filed for the divorce, claimed that the two had not spoken in over two years.

There was an interesting twist involving Detective Andrus. Andrus' son was an attorney. Mrs. Munckton was indigent so the county was required to appoint an attorney to represent her. Young Andrus was given the case. One might wonder about a possible conflict of interest between having the father as the investigator and the son as the defender. Apprehension was eliminated when, during the trial, defense attorney Andrus went after his father and the way he obtained the confession. Andrus the attorney was able to prove that the confession was made under duress and without counsel present. There is no report about how Andrus family get-togethers went after that.

Without TV or radio to serve as a distraction, murder trials held a strong entertainment appeal. Usually, it was men who attended; however, if the case involved a woman there were frequently some females in attendance. In the trial of Hattie Munckton, those in the gallery and lining the walls were mostly women and there were even some girls present. There were times during the trial when decorum required that the ladies cover their ears. As people feel compelled to peek today, they probably listened to the testimony then.

Prosecution

The prosecution had a very straight forward case. There were several doctors who would testify that Munckton had died as the result of a shotgun wound (cause). There was also a confession, the weapon, and a motive of continual discord in the family. If there was a problem with the admissibility of the written confession, the prosecution also had a series of respected people who would testify that Hattie had admitted verbally to killing her husband.

As the trial began, it looked like the prosecution's case would be further supported by the couple's son, George. He was one of their key witnesses placed on the stand to tell of the behavior of the family. While he was on the stand, George's testimony was basically against the whole family. Although he was not considered to have championed his mother's cause, the day after George was a witness he moved his seat from in the gallery to a chair next to his mother; a demonstration of support.

During George's testimony an interesting story emerged. He told of Officer Hubbs offering him money if his mother was convicted. Where the money was to come from was never made clear. The offer would have had to have happened while George was at his paternal grandparent's. This may have explained why George was moved to the juvenal center.

The prosecution knew going in to the trial that they had the possibility of an emotional issue. Their fear was the possibility that a jury would feel sympathy for the defendant.

Defense

The defense had to overcome the confession and turn the case into one of justifiable homicide. Their first strategy was to try to have the confession that Hattie signed the night her husband died, ruled inadmissible. The argument Attorney Andrus used was based on the confession being obtained under duress. When that failed they had a witness, Mrs. Morehead, who testified that Hattie had been given a large amount of alcohol to calm her. The implication was that she was under the influence. When she was on the stand Hattie would acknowledge that she did not know what she had signed.

In all trials there is the question of whether the defendant should testify in his or her own defense. Many lawyers feel that the defendant's own words usually have a negative impact on the jury. In this case Hattie's testimony would help her cause. Small and diminutive, Hattie's day and a half as a witness allowed her to detail the constant verbal and physical abuse under which she had lived for years. Her story rang a loud bell among the jurors. During the trial there was even a graphic story of how Munckton performed an involuntary abortion on his wife, and then he proceeded to beat her when she did not work hard enough in a field three days later.

The trial lasted five days. With the exception of George, the prosecution's witnesses testified almost exclusively as to the fact that it was a murder and Hattie's numerous admissions of guilt. George was the only prosecution witness who testified about the relationships within the family. Interestingly, not one member of Munckton family was called by the prosecution to testify as to incidents they had witnessed. Had they been called, Munckton may not have appeared as evil as he was portrayed by everyone else.

In contrast, the defense's witnesses almost exclusively testified as to acts of violence they had witnessed and the relationship within the family. The witnesses were mostly Hattie's relatives but their tales were those of miserable people who lived under a dark cloud of violence. For sympathy, Hattie had her mother come into court. Weak and frail, Mrs. Cameron added an emotional element as she struggled into a seat next to her daughter.

A twist

There was one unsubstantiated claim that a witness made during the trial. According to Fred Cameron, Hattie's brother, a couple of years before the shooting, Munckton had bragged that he (Munckton) had killed a railroad watchman in Schenectady. The incident with the watchman had happened while Munckton, along with a gang he worked with, were planning to rob some materials from a boxcar. According to the tale, Munckton told

Cameron that his role was to take out the watchman, so he hit him with a coupling pin. Munckton told Cameron he had never mentioned it for fear he would be arrested.

The prosecution attacked Cameron's story asking why he never reported the alleged confession to the authorities. Cameron pointed out that he never reported any of Munckton's actions to the authorities – meaning the acts against his own sister.

It is not obvious exactly when the prosecution realized the effect Hattie was having on the jury. What is clear is that her cross-examination was unusually short as if they wanted her off the stand.

The prosecution only put three rebuttal witnesses on the stand and they only addressed two peripheral issues raised by the defense. The first was Mrs. Morehead, Hattie's sister, who had given her the brandy on the night she made the confession. The purpose of her rebuttal testimony was to show that the amount of alcohol Hattie consumed would not have made the signing of the confession the act of a drunken woman.

Since Hattie had claimed the windows were nailed shut and, therefore, she could not escape the house, two other witnesses were called to testify about securing the windows the day after the shooting. The both men testified that they had secured the house by nailing the doors and windows closed from the outside. When the defense questioned the two, neither could say positively if the windows were already nailed from the inside.

What the prosecution did not do was to put on any rebuttal witnesses regarding the abuse. Many people who had witnessed the attacks or bruises were named by Hattie in her testimony. The prosecution did not place even one on the stand to say that Hattie had lied about how Munckton had treated her.

The closings

The closing arguments were based almost exclusively on the issue of abuse. The real question that the jury would have to deal with was the believability of Mrs. Munckton.

Although the defense's closing would take thirty minutes, Andrus summarized the extent of the abuse in a few sentences. "Never has a woman been accorded so cruel treatment for so many years as has Mrs. Munckton. If the wife or sister of any man in this jury box had been treated one-half as cruelly as has Mrs. Munckton, you too would have taken the law in your own hands and would be standing here today accused of murder."

McKnight's summary for the prosecution would take three quarters of an hour but would drive to the point of believability. McKnight made his opinion very clear. "I have been engaged in some twenty murder trials, and in all that time I have never listened to a defense so preposterous, so unnatural, so revolting, as has been put forth in this case. She has told a story beyond parallel in any in history. No writer of fiction has ever drawn on his imagination to the extent of this defendant." One has to wonder how McKnight's words played on an all male jury.

At 5:45 on Saturday evening, the case was given to the jury. Believing that the deliberations would take some time, the court ordered that blankets be brought in so the jurors would be able to take a nap.

At about midnight there was a real scare. One of the jurors had gotten sick and there was a chance that there would need to be a retrial. Judge Rockwood asked the man if he could possibly stay on. The juror agreed to try if the judge could provide a place to lie down and a bigger room in which the group could deliberate. A couch was brought into the supervisors' chambers and jury continued.

The first indications of where the jury stood were at 4:30 in the morning when the jury came back into the courtroom and asked for further instructions as to justifiable homicide.

The Verdict

At 5:00 in the morning the jury sent the bailiff to tell the judge that they had reached a decision. At 5:05 in the morning everyone was assembled in the courtroom.

The twelve member jury had agreed that it was justifiable homicide.

There was, however, yet to be seen the expression of the sincerity of the verdict. Hattie almost fainted when she stood before the court and heard the news. From her seat there appeared for the first time in four days a smile across her "careworn face." Rather than leaving the court immediately, Hattie stayed at her seat and accepted the congratulations of those who had been present at that early hour to hear the news. A unique event occurred. After they were dismissed by Judge Rockwood, each juror went to Hattie, shook her hand and told her they were glad she was free. Tears were actually seen in some of the men's eyes.

The trial was so interesting that those who had been there at that early hour to hear the verdict almost all stayed for two more hours to discuss the case.

An aside

Hattie's father had fared less well. On the last day of her trial her father was called into another courtroom in the same building. It was time for him to be sentenced for his bigamy conviction. He was sent to Dannamora Prison for a year.

Afterward

Hattie left that morning on a train for her sister's house in Schenectady to rest. A few days later she went to her brother's in Amsterdam. When she arrived in Amsterdam she was greeted by a large group of supporters who gave her an ovation. Arriving at her brother's house, there was a second crowd and a second ovation. Apparently the excitement was too much for Hattie and a week after the trail she was confined to her bed with a severe cold.

A week after the trial, Hattie's sister-in-law came back to Ballston Spa to retrieve the property that had been taken from the house. Apparently, while Hattie was in jail awaiting trial, two horses, five cows, eight pigs, and sixty chickens had disappeared along with the contents of the house.

At the same time of her sister-in-laws visit, it was learned that fourteen year-old George Munckton was missing [he had had a birthday]. His mother had no idea where he had gone, although they assumed that some member of the Munckton family had taken him.

Mrs. Burt

"If I die, I will die in sin."

There are tales, and there are tales, but there is no better tale than the one that has but one who can tell it.

To those who have not experienced the nights as they near the winter solstice in the northeast, be assured they are always long and usually cold. The night of December 15/16, 1880, was no exception to this rule. In just a few days it would be officially winter, thus it was within a few minutes of the longest night of the year. An optimist would probably refer to that day as the shortest day of the year but then again who could be an optimist and still write true crime stories?

Within the first dark cold hour after midnight, four gunshots were heard coming from a small cottage in North Albany. Moments later a woman dressed only in her nightclothes ran out the front door of the house. Cold and frightened she ran into a neighbor's house not even taking the time to knock. In her heart she felt that the reason she was frightened justified her leaving her two young children in the house from which she had just fled. Then again what she had seen made her realize they were not in imminent danger.

Instinctively, she had run to the residence of hotel manager Nelson Rivenburgh. It was a place she considered safe and safe was a key factor for her at the time.

The combination of gunshots and the sound of a person downstairs had woken Rivenburgh from a sound sleep. When he got downstairs Rivenburgh was confronted by the hysterical woman. He took the woman into his parlor where he tried to calm her enough that she could tell her story.

Gasping for breath, it took several moments for the woman to relate to her neighbors the events that had generated her leaving her home and children. It was an account based in fear, deceit and laced with gaps so large that they could be depicted as craters. Although everyone wanted to believe the woman, her account would raise questions that were never fully answered: at least not to everyone's satisfaction. Believe the story or not those who knew the cast of characters involved in the incident were satisfied with the outcome.

Rivenburgh had listened to the woman's narrative realizing instantly the gravity of the situation. Through the woman's emotional words he had learned enough about what had transpired in the cottage that he knew he had to go inside to check on the situation. He also knew that he didn't want to enter the source of the shots alone. When the woman was calmed, Rivenburgh hurried from his house and banged on the doors of his neighbor's houses. After he had collected two other neighbors, he was ready to enter the woman's cottage.

Rivenburgh and his companions cautiously approached the home at 26 Genesee Street. The small group was logically anxious. If what the woman had reported was correct, they were in no immanent danger; however, they understood that what they might find would be troubling.

They walked through the entry hall and to the kitchen, which was at the end of the hall in the back of the house. Although warned, none of the men who entered the house were prepared for the sight that they were about to confront. There, lying on the floor was the body of a woman who hours before would have been considered beautiful, perhaps even stunning. Her eyes were slightly open. The men could tell, by the amount of blood surrounding her body, (all of which had escaped from a wound in her head) that she had breathed her last.

Over by the woodstove there was a man, the sight of whom made their stomachs turn over. Like the woman on the floor, he had also been shot in the head but there was much more damage from his wounds than those of the woman. The man's wounds were so serious that portions of the contents of his skull were visible near him on the floor.

The men noticed how much like a family setting it still was with plates and food left on the table from dinner.

It is only natural, that with all the revulsion that was present, that each of the three men who had entered the kitchen would later remember the situation differently. One would swear that the man was dead when they entered. Another said that despite his wounds the man lived for a couple of breaths after they arrived. The third, perhaps because he was so rattled by the scene before him, was unsure of the status of the man's life.

During the remainder of the night that followed, the woman who had run out of the house told all of them and others who were to gather in the cottage the same tale. She told of how the man had become angry with his girlfriend and immersed in his anger shot her. According to the survivor, the man then turned the gun on himself firing **three shots** into his own head.

There are many stories of people who have committed suicide by shooting themselves, but few where the person was so determined as to fire three times into his own head. The act was even more chilling because to fire the hand gun used required two separate actions. Unlike today's handguns in which pulling the trigger both cocks the gun and fires it, the gun the man had used required that the hammer be pulled back by the thumb then the gun was fired by pulling the trigger.

Winter 1880

In mid-December the weather in Albany usually looked like a Currier and Ives painting with horse drawn sleighs being pulled over the snow covered streets. In December 1880, the weather in the northeast had turned unusually mild for several days. It was so unseasonably warm that the newspapers noted that only wheeled vehicles could be seen on the muddy streets. The snow had melted so extensively that the sleighs and cutters had all been returned to the sheds where they had spent the summer.

The unseasonably warm weather brought with it both benefits and detriments. Although Christmas shopping was nothing like the phenomenon it is today, the mild weather did allow shoppers to visit the downtown stores with fewer layers of clothing. Conversely, the ice harvest, so important to the region's economy, would be greatly diminished by the warm temperatures.

It was the days of the icebox. People had learned to keep food in the summer by placing it in a wooden cabinet that had one section built to hold ice. This was the precursor to the modern refrigerator. The ice used in New York City was harvested along the Hudson and in the frozen lakes of the Adirondacks. Ice was an essential mainstay of the region's economy. It was obvious that the mild temperatures were going to cause the economy of the region to suffer this year. For the men who earned a portion of the annual income harvesting the ice, the impact was already being predicted. The following summer it would be felt by those speculators and merchants who shipped and sold the ice.

An evening out

Perhaps it was the mild weather that made the man, who now lay dead on the floor, to think the romantic thoughts of spring. This would have explained his impetuous decision to pick up his girlfriend for an evening out. Then again his reason may have been nothing more than a need for a drink. Or perhaps it was just that he wanted to go out for a social evening. Whatever his initial motives, on Wednesday, December 15th, Charles Burt went out for his last evening on the town.

Burt, who was thirty years old, was too young for this to be his last night out. He was the reasonably wealthy son of a local Albany brewer, Uri Burt. According to rumor, he was also the nephew of former Governor Lucius Robinson. Although Robinson had been defeated for re-election the previous year, the impact of his name was still felt in Albany.

Too handsome for his own good, Charles Burt was of medium height and build. When not drinking, Burt was considered to have an exceptional personality. Charles Burt was obviously proud of his looks trying to make the most with them. In a period when most married men wore beards, he was clean-shaven. From a well-connected family he had all the social graces of the Victorian Era, that is, when he wanted to exhibit them. In some people's eyes Charles was quite the ladies man. One of those who was less enamored by this perception was his wife. A becoming woman in her own right, Mrs. Burt was the woman who had run from the cottage. She was the adopted daughter of one of the wealthier families of suburban Loudonville.

A few years before the tragedy reported here, Charles had been standing and talking with his father on the steps of the family's brewery. Suddenly and inexplicably, in the moments the two were on the steps, a part of the roof came loose and fell on Charles' father. His father was seriously injured and died a short time later. There are losses, but few deeper felt than that of a loved one whose death was both tragic and occurred while a loved one looked on.

Charles Burt had for some time (probably two years) had been engaged in a relationship with a woman who was known by two names, Sarah Travers and Kate Smith. It was generally held that her real name was Kate Smith. She was the woman found on the floor of the cottage. Although early reports would imply that Kate was a woman who earned her living by letting men enjoy the pleasure of her company, it is more probable that she worked as a domestic. The various descriptions of Kate are examples of where what those who want gossip and what was true are not the same.

Charles was always popular, hanging with a group of young men who were all from wealthy families. After five years of marriage, around 1878, Charles Burt's wife had become aware of her husband's relationship with Kate and they separated. In an unusual turn, the wife moved in with her husband's widowed mother. This may have been because her mother-in-law lived in a comfortable house at 797 Broadway in Albany or it could have been that the women had both experienced the loss of a man who they trusted and loved.

The legal situation of the couple's separation had made it through the first steps of a court resolution. According to the judge's order, Mrs. Burt, the wife, had won temporary payments from Charles to the tune of $20 a week in support for their children. The size of the settlement reflects the worth of the family, as this was in a time when working class families usually lived on less than $6 a week.

Charles Burt's mother remarried a short time after her son's separation. Charles' wife and children moved with his mother and her new husband to New York City. As the family's luck would have it, his mother's second husband died soon after the marriage. The two Burt women and the two children returned to Albany.

After several discussions, Charles and his wife agreed to try reconciliation. They moved into the cottage on Genesee Street. It appears that despite Charles' claims that he would not see Kate, the relationship rekindled.

Sarah "Kate" Travers' life was a very different story than Charles'. She had been born not on the other side of the tracks, but even further away on the social spectrum - on the other side of the mountain. Doctors, who examined her after her death, told of her form as being that of perfection (are a rare description in Victorian autopsies). The New York Times used the term "siren" to describe Kate probably as a reflection of her beauty and of her seeming power over Charles. It is entirely probable that, based on the social status, Kate was too beautiful for her own good or at the very least for her own ability to deal with the ramifications of such beauty. In death the reporters noted that her long black hair swung freely from the table the men in the neighborhood had placed her on. Her dark hair contrasted perfectly with her pale almost pure white skin. Those who saw Kate after she died all agreed she looked much younger than her 26 years.

Probably in an effort to discredit Kate it was published that Charles' name had been written in pencil on one of her breasts. Then again the couple may have had some unique sexual practices. In any event it was exactly the type of news that those whose greatest pleasures in life come from judging and condemning others waited to hear.

Witness?

There was really only one witness to the events in that small cottage that evening. That witness was Charles' wife and what follows is the story as she told it.

In front of the coroner Mrs. Burt told how her husband had had dinner with his family. A few hours later, he had gone out for the evening. She went on to say that about midnight she heard a man and a woman whispering outside the house. Assuming it was Charles, she got out of her bed and went to the window to see what was happening. Peeking through the sashes she saw that her conjecture was correct, the man's voice did belong to her husband. Through the window she heard her husband say, "When she unlocks the door, you come in."

Ready for a confrontation, Mrs. Burt, who recognized Kate, went to the front door and said through the glass, "I will open the door for you but not for her."

According to Mrs. Burt, before she had a chance to unlock the door her husband burst through. In the entry hall, Mrs. Burt stood frozen in fear. It was then that her husband announced, "I will shoot you for this." Frightened by her husband's threat and, knowing his propensity toward violence, Mrs. Burt ran upstairs. In part, her reaction would have been to protect herself but it would also have been instinctive for her, as a mother, to want to protect her two young children. Both children were sleeping in the upper floor bedrooms. It was while his wife was upstairs, that Charles went into to the couple's bedroom on the first floor. It was his practice to hide a handgun between the mattress and springs of the couple's bed. According to Mrs. Burt, after finding the revolver he went back outside where he rejoined Kate. The wife, hearing him leave the house, came back downstairs to try to secure the door and keep the couple and the problems they represented out.

Minutes later Charles returned, this time he brought his paramour into the house. There is no account of how he got in through the secured door, but Mrs. Burt stressed that once inside he locked the door behind himself. How he did this after breaking the lock the first time is not clear (this is her story and not always logical).

Back in the house Charles and Kate, who were both quite drunk, stumbled to the kitchen, in the back of the house. For reason's she would never explain the wife followed the couple to the doorway of the kitchen. There was a conflict in the testimony that followed. According to several reports, Mrs. Burt said that her husband shut the kitchen door behind himself. She said that then she listened through the door. If that is the case she had a lot of detail about what happened out of her sight. In other reports the door was open and she saw what transpired. To believe the detail that would follow one has to believe that the door was open.

According to Mrs. Burt, Kate tried to take the pistol away from her lover. Burt retaliated by hitting her with the gun. Mrs. Burt said that her husband then turned to Kate and said, "I have been playing underhanded work with you these past two weeks." (They had been involved for two years, not two weeks, although that may have been how long the relationship had been refreshed.) He went on to say, "There will be no more of it."

Mrs. Burt then saw (or heard) her husband and Travers whisper several times to each other. She told everyone that she was unable to hear exactly what they said during this exchange. Finally, Charles told Travers to get down on her knees and pray. He repeated this demand three or four times. Travers refused to kneel or pray saying, "No. If I die, I will die in sin." Travers then backed up a step and leaned on a bureau that was kept in the kitchen. In her last moments Travers was standing about four feet away from Burt.

Charles Burt then said, "Are you ready?"

Calmly Travers responded, "Yes, if you want to fire."

Mrs. Burt told the coroner's jury how upon hearing the word "fire" her husband had shot Travers once in the head. Travers fell immediately to the floor.

According to Mrs. Burt, after Charles had shot Kate, he turned, looked at her and shot the gun three times. Charles never said a word to his wife after he shot Kate. Rather, he just pulled the trigger three times. One might have assumed that after the first or second shot the pain would have overcome the drunkenness, but who's being logical.

Asked if Charles had ever brought "the woman" to the house prior to that evening, Mrs. Burt said, "No." She went on to say, however, that, "He had brought her to the house at 797 Broadway." That was his mother's house.

There are two very real problems with the story told by Mrs. Burt. First, how had Charles been able to lock the door when he entered with Sarah; remember she said he had broken the lock when he entered the first time? Second how was he able to pull the trigger three times, while shooting himself in the head? The second question plagued the people who read the story.

Over the next two days the newspapers and probably Burt's family would try to explain Charles' shooting accomplishment. This search for an explanation may have been fueled by the Burt family's social standing in the community and the close relationship of Mrs. Burt and her mother-in-law.

The autopsies that followed tried to address the question of the three shots. In reading the reports one must note that the Burts were a family of means and of considerable political influence. At the time of the shooting there were strong political pressures in Victorian Albany. These influences would have been imbedded in this case and probably manipulated the final report.

It was quickly determined that Kate had died of a single

bullet to the brain. Her death was as the neighbors reported, almost immediate.

The newspapers were careful to point out the names of three doctors who were present for the autopsy of Charles. In order to have the account believed the Burts needed as many credible witnesses as possible so the reports noted that other, unnamed physicians were present as witnesses. Charles' revolver held five bullets and that four had been fired. The number of shots fired was in agreement with the story told by Mrs. Burt. According to the coroner's report, only three of the bullets ever hit a person. One had hit Sarah. A second had wounded Charles above the right eye. The third had hit Charles above the right ear causing tremendous damage. The fourth shot hit the wall in the kitchen. The doctors said that his death was almost instant. The doctors' findings are in direct conflict with the reports of the three men who entered the house who said that Charles was still breathing when they got to the kitchen; however, the doctors' findings would have been reassuring to the family.

On December 27th, some 11 days after the affair began (the shooting occurred in the early morning hours of the 16th) the coroner's jury in Albany met to make its final report. After some deliberations, the inquest determined that Sarah Travers (Kate Smith) had died as the result of a bullet fired by Charles A. Burt.

The true identity of the woman who was shot was not clear even two weeks after the incident. The Troy Press carried a brief article in late December that said she was the wife of a former hack driver from Gloversville, named Traverse. This report noted that the Traverse couple had moved from Gloversville to Mayfield, where her husband had gone into the lumber business. At the time of her autopsy it was believed he was living in the woods of the Adirondacks and had not heard of her death. In a true editorial on Victorian values the newspaper noted that, "Mrs. Traverse is represented to have been a very beautiful young woman, but easily flattered and cajoled. It was through her vanity that she fell, and ever since her course has been downward." Earlier reports had the surname as Travers and that it was her father, not her husband, who was in the logging business. The early reports stated that her father was the owner of a lumber mill in Cranberry Creek, Fulton County.

It was also reported that her parents believed that she was married to Burt. The exact details are not accessible.

Investigation

The investigation found that at the time of the shooting Sarah was employed as a "domestic" at 68 Chapel Street, in Albany. The evening of the 15th Sarah had asked permission of her employer to go out. At 9:00 she and Burt returned to her employer's house. She introduced Charles to her employers as Charles Van Alstyne (interestingly this was the maiden name of Rivenburgh's wife). The family Sarah worked for believed Burt was intoxicated when they were introduced. Soon after 9:00 the couple left the house. Over the next two hours they were seen in several taverns on Green Street, a neighborhood that did not enjoy the best reputation in the city. It was believed that the couple was intoxicated when they took the last trolley north that fateful evening.

There was a pertinent point that was not explained. According to Mrs. Burt and others who were in kitchen following the shooting, the table was still covered with the dinner dishes. If the family ate together, and Mrs. Burt was any kind of Victorian wife, why had she not at least cleared the table? Was the truth more like Charles brought his girlfriend home where they made snacks for themselves? Mrs. Burt, hearing a noise in the kitchen, took the gun out from under the mattress and went to investigate. Finding her husband and his lover in the kitchen, someone began shooting.

The exact details of this story will never be found today. What it does show is the political influence of some families. Even more important, it shows an underlying value of the Victorian era. It was the unwritten practice of the time that if a person did not deserve to live, their death could almost always be overlooked. Once the spice of the affair had run its course and all the winking of one eye had been completed, Mrs. Burt could go on with her life. After all, she had been married to a man who had emotionally, if not physically, abused her.

Mary Rogers

"The truth has not been told"

Author's note: this story took place between 1902 and 1905, a time when yellow journalism was near its zenith. The stories carried in the newspapers during this period were sensational and often more the editor's opinions or perspective than totally factual accounts. Even newspapers that considered themselves to be legitimate, when they tried to correct the stories carried, the tabloids often went too far in the opposite direction. The problem of sorting between the diversely different perspectives of this story was compounded by the nature of the incident - a murder story that featured a woman. Then, as today, women in crime tended to capture and hold the public's attention.

Adding to the problem of finding what transpired in this story is the social environment. It was a time when young farm girls were moving into villages and cities to obtain work in the mills. Parents were worried about the associations their daughters would make living on their own. Stories such as this one allowed parents to discuss with (preach to) their daughters the potential downfall of a good girl caught up in the questionable morals of a city. This moral element in this story made the truth more elusive.

Although the man had a reason to be looking, the body was found more by accident than as part of an organized search. Left in a river near a mill on the edge of town, one would have expected the discovery to have been much sooner. After all, the place was selected so the body could be found and found quickly.

On Wednesday evening, Payson Hathaway was on his way to work when he noticed a hat with a note pinned in the hatband hanging on a tree. The note read, "blame no one as i have at last put an end to my miserable life as my wife nows i have ever threatened it, every body nows I have not enything or no body to live for, no one came blame me and so blame no one as my last request. Marcus Rogers". [The spelling and grammar are as in the note.] Curiosity raised, Hathaway took the hat to the police who considered the note a joke and did not follow up. Not wanting to take something that did not belong to him, Hathaway took the hat back and retied it to the same tree.

The next morning Samuel Jewett noticed the hat. Unlike Hathaway, Jewett walked through the small grove to the bank of the Walloomsac River. There, less than two feet from the shore, lying in a little over a foot of water, he noticed something that looked like a log resting on the bottom of the river. It was hard to identify what it was because it was nearly covered by sand. Looking more closely Jewett realized it was the body of a person laying face downward. Jewett took the same note and hat to the police that Hathaway had taken the night before. This time, however, in addition to the hat and note, Jewett reported that he was sure he found a body in the river. Several men, including two police officers and a village selectman, went to investigate Jewett's report.

It did not take long to pull the body out of the water and place it on the bank to dry. Despite the note, the first examination of the body indicated few signs of a suicide. The face had several scratches; there was a serious bruise over the right eye and the man's ear was badly torn. With the note found on Wednesday and the body on Thursday it was apparent that the corpse had been in the water for at least a full day.

A search of the man's pockets found some insurance papers, slightly over two dollars in cash and a silver watch. It was a small bounty to show for a life of hard work. The watch, which would not have been waterproof, had stopped at 12:30 giving some indication of the time the body went in the water.

Taking the body home

The papers in the pocket provided the name Marcus Rogers. It was soon learned that a Mary Rogers was boarding with the Perham family on Safford Street. The officers remembered that Mary had been to the station the day before to report her husband was missing; she even suspected that he had committed suicide. The men who found the body decided to bring the body to the house where Mary was staying. When they arrived carrying the dead body, Mary acknowledged she was married to a Marcus – now a corpse. The marriage was somewhat of a surprise to the Mrs. Perham with whom Mary was living. Mrs. Perham had been led to believe Marcus was Mary's brother- not her husband. In the days that followed, various members of the Perham family would give different dates of when they had learned Mary was married. If she did not know Mary was married until the corpse arrived, Mrs. Laura Perham would have been the last member in the family to know.

As the men with the body tried to take it inside, Mary said that she was only a boarder and did not feel it appropriate to have Marcus' body in the house. She asked the men who were carrying the remains if the village would pay for the burial. The selectman in the group assured her that was not an option. She then suggested that it be taken to his aunts' house a couple of blocks away. The men told her that was not an option either. Finally, she suggested that the best place was his brother's house in Hoosick Falls – after all Marcus had been employed there as a farmer. The men, who were not going to take the body two blocks away, were definitely not going to take it 10 miles to the brother's. The problem was resolved when Mary talked to Mrs. Perham and assured her that Marcus was insured and as the beneficiary she would pay for the funeral. Finally, the men were allowed to bring the body into the Safford Street house.

Having slipped on not following up on Hathaway's finding of the note on Wednesday, the police became more careful in their investigation. They started by asking Mary the questions that follow any suspicious death. Their preliminary inquiry focused on when she last saw her husband and under what circumstances.

Mary explained that she had seen her husband early Tuesday evening. The meeting had ended in a fight with Marcus throwing his life insurance receipt book at her. Mary said that when he threw the book he yelled, "I'll go and kill myself." She told the officers that she considered the comment an idle threat. When asked when she had gone to bed on the night in question Mary responded, "About 9:00." That would have been 3 1/2 hours before the watch stopped.

Deputy Sheriff Nash, the first officer involved, was puzzled. Mary had come to the town hall the day before to report her husband missing. On that occasion Mary said that she had come at the behest of his aunt (the one that lived two blocks away). In Mary's report that her husband was missing she had made some unusual comments. First, she had said that she believed that her husband had drowned himself (few people use drowning as a way to commit suicide). She had gone on to say she believed his body would be discovered within the town's limits – it was. When asked what she expected the town officials to do, Mary told the officer that she felt it would be appropriate to ring the fire bell and have the firemen search for the body (not her husband, his body).

As the body was finally being carried into the house, Mary claimed that after her request for a community wide search was turned down by the police, she had spent all day Wednesday looking for Marcus. Her assertion of searching did little to mollify the officer's anxiety.

Autopsy

In the living room of the Perham's house, two doctors performed an autopsy on Marcus Rogers. To characterize Mary's behavior during the procedure as unusual would be an understatement. She did not even leave the room while her former husband was being dissected. Instead of grieving or even walking away from the grisly sight, Mary chose to converse with the doctors and officers who were present.

Whenever a body is found in water, the logical assumption is that the person drowned. Yet, during the procedure, Mary repeatedly asked the doctors if they had found any signs of poison.

The results of the preliminary autopsy were both telling

and left open some questions. Marcus' lungs were filled with air so his death was not the result of drowning. An examination showed that despite the injury above his eye there was no apparent severe damage to the brain – the skull was damaged. Those results left open the possibility a death by trauma or poison, so Marcus' brain, stomach and other organs were sent to a lab in Burlington for forensic examination.

Inquiry

The afternoon the body was found an official inquiry was convened. The inquiry, called a coroner's jury, was charged with examining the circumstances surrounding Marcus' death and rendering a verdict as to the cause.

The cast

In 1902, even more than today, Bennington was a small, close-knit village. It was one of those communities where everyone may not have known everyone else but given some diligence, in half an hour they could find out about anyone who lived in town. The problem then, as now, is that what one finds out through the grapevine is not always accurate.

Since there was the probability of a murder, Deputy Nash was joined in the investigation by Deputy Godfrey. The officers soon learned that Mary had a close female friend in the village named Stella Bates. The two women had met when they both roomed at the same house on East Main Street. Bates, like Mary, was not a native of Bennington. From what was learned it appeared both women had moved into the village the previous spring seeking work. Neither woman appeared to have any close family living in the village, although Mary Rogers had some links through her deceased husband.

Although Bates was harder to get a handle on, the officer soon learned that neither woman enjoyed a stellar reputation. In the case of Mrs. Mary Rogers, the deputies were told that although she may have been married, she had been seen in the company of at least one other man (the rumors alleged the possibility of even more).

There was also a rather troubling story uncovered. It seems that the previous fall the Rogers had lost a six month old baby girl under suspicious circumstances.

At least some of these stories the officers heard came from Laura Perham, in whose house Mary rented a room. To characterize Mrs. Perham as nervous when questioned by the deputies would have been a gross understatement; she was panicky.

The testimony at the inquest that began the day the body was found was overseen by justice of the peace Shutleff, who had been called upon to administer the coroner's jury. Shutleff decided that to avoid corroboration, witnesses would not be allowed to hear the testimony given by other witnesses. He ordered that all potential witnesses be held in a separate room and brought before the jury when it was his or her turn to answer questions.

The testimonies of the first several witnesses were rather mundane. They told of Marcus being seen in Bennington during the day on Tuesday, July 12th; however, none of the witnesses claimed to have seen him after 8:00 that evening. According to the witnesses, Marcus claimed to have over twenty-four dollars with him on the day in question. It was also learned that he carried a life insurance policy worth $500 and was in the practice of carrying the payment book on his person. Two of Marcus's aunts and his brother told the coroner's jury that he was in the village that fateful day in the hopes of reconciling with his wife.

During the hearing it came out that 32 year-old Marcus and 19 year-old Mary had been married for three and a half years. That made him 28 and her 16 at the time of their wedding. The couple had separated the previous January in an effort to pay off their excessive debts. Marcus had gone to work on his brother's farm in Hoosick and Mary taken a series of positions as a domestic. Marcus, at least, had hoped to get back together when the debts were settled.

There was a real doubt about the reality of reconciliation. Several witnesses, mostly members of Marcus' family, testified to the numerous arguments between the couple. According to those who testified, these disagreements had been ongoing for years. Several other witnesses politely told of Mary's interest in playing the role of a single person (one she had taken on in Bennington). The quality of the men she saw may not have been outstanding and the list was not short.

In the case of a mysterious death, the spouse is always a

central figure in the investigation. Everyone present at the hearing could not wait to hear Mary's explanation of what had occurred. On the stand she told how she and Marcus had lost their only child, explaining that she was home alone with the six month old child when it fell and hit its head. [Marcus' family would later say that Mary dropped the baby on its head.] The baby's accident had happened about noon. Mary had laid the child down and when she checked on it at 3:00 that afternoon the child was dead.

Mary went on to tell of how a few months later Marcus needed work. He had asked his brother, William, for a position. William offered him a job on his farm but said that "he would have nothing for Mary to do." Mary and Marcus agreed to separate until they could pay off the debts they had incurred. Mary took a position as a domestic in Hoosick Falls and Marcus went to work for his brother on a farm a mile out of that village.

Mary's first position was as a domestic in the house of a Mrs. Corcoran. The position ended when Mary's employer died. A short time later, Mary moved to Bennington where in her brief stay she held at least three different positions as a domestic. It is not clear why Mary kept losing her positions but the general consensus was that it was her social habits. Mary had been unemployed for at least the month preceding her husband's death.

Mary went on to confirm the rumor that on Tuesday the 12th, Marcus had come to Bennington in hopes that she would reconsider his numerous offers and join him on his brother's farm. She said she could not get back together until after the bills were paid off.

Mary told how when the two met on Tuesday evening, Marcus became very upset when she told him that she would not "take up housekeeping." She told how he was so depressed that he said he would end his life. Mary went on to say that she took little notice because it was a threat he had used several times in an effort to get her to come back to him. It was obvious to those who heard her testify, that what Mary lacked in morals she made up for in ego.

Mary went on to say that she had gone to bed at 9:00 on Tuesday evening and had arisen at 6:00 the next morning. Mary confirmed that on Wednesday she had gone to Marcus' aunts' to see if he had spent the night there. She claimed that she was surprised by the news that Marcus had not returned to his aunts' house as expected. Mary said that when she learned Marcus was missing, she told the authorities, then had spent the entire day looking for him.

Even early in the investigation much of Mary's story was not corroborated.

The inquest went from interesting to fascinating in just moments when 24 year-old Boyd Perham took the stand. It was as though the room took on the atmosphere of the old Perry Mason books and television series.

Boyd was the Perham's elder son; there was a second son, 19 year-old Leon. Both boys still resided with their parents and, therefore, in the same house with Mary Rogers. With virtually no prodding Boyd told the inquest how a few months before (he was unsure of the exact date), Mary Rogers had offered him $500, the same amount as the insurance policy, if he would go to Hoosick Corners and eliminate Marcus Rogers. When Boyd refused her offer, Mary started to "work on" his younger brother Leon.

After Boyd told about being approached to eliminate Marcus, his testimony changed direction completely with him telling the incidents the night that Marcus went missing. The story Boyd related was as his brother, Leon, had told it to him (this was technically hearsay but it was an inquest, not a trial). According to Boyd's statement, Marcus Rogers had agreed to meet his wife at Morgan's Grove (a small grove on the north side of the Walloomsac River that flows through Bennington). Supposedly, when Marcus arrived at the agreed rendezvous he found that Leon was there with Mary. Boyd said that he understood that the conversation that followed was congenial and that Marcus agreed to have his hands tied as part of a magic trick. When Marcus was bound, the couple placed a handkerchief soaked with chloroform over Marcus' nose and mouth. Marcus had struggled but because he was tied, the two were able to overpower him. Boyd went on to say that when Marcus was finally unconscious, Mary and his brother had rolled the body into the river. Boyd's explanation might explain the scratches found on Marcus' face.

Boyd went on to say that the Mary had been working on

the details of her plan to be rid of Marcus for several months. When questioned about where Mary had obtained the chloroform, Leon said that it was purchased by Stella Bates who, like himself, knew all about the plan.

Although there were common threads, the details of what happened to Marcus Rogers had changed with each witness at the inquest. Those in attendance expected that when Leon took the stand in his own defense, the story would develop yet another twist. Such was not to be the case. When asked questions about his brother's testimony, Leon confirmed the story with virtually no changes. Through his testimony, Leon Perham confessed to being an accessory to murder. Leon did, however, make a point of stressing that Stella Bates was not present at the time of the murder.

The inquest would continue but based on the testimony up to that point, Sutleff ordered that Mary, Stella, and Leon be arrested immediately.

When Mrs. Perham took the stand her testimony was confused and cyclic. It is not clear if her confusion was the result of the stress of having two sons involved in a murder; from her own intellectual limits; or the stress of speaking in a public setting. Mrs. Perham told the coroner's jury that on Wednesday (the day after the murder) she had seen Mary burn letters in the family's woodstove. Mrs. Perham was not sure exactly how many letters were destroyed but guessed that it was approximately six. Mrs. Perham went on to say that on that same day, before the body was found, that Mary had told her she was sure Marcus had committed suicide and did not know what she would do with the body when it was found. Asked why she had not come forward sooner, Mrs. Perham said it was because she feared for her own life. She was the only person at the hearing who expressed a fear of Mary.

Morris Knapp, another of the Perham's boarders, was also called as a witness. Knapp testified to having taken Mary "a number of times" by carriage to visit Marcus at William Rogers' farm. Knapp testified that at the time of the drives he believed that Marcus was Mary's brother. Knapp said that he was kept in the dark about Marcus and Mary's relationship because their conversations were at a distance and he could not hear. Knapp maintained that Mary never talked to him about the contents of her conversations with Marcus. Knapp went on to say that Mary had told him that in early July she had gone to Hoosick Falls to be present when Marcus had married.

According to Knapp, Mary had asked him to marry her. His report of the proposal is too romantic not to be included. "She asked me if I'd as soon marry her." He went on, "I told her, 'as soon as anyone, but, I was not ready to get married.'"

Knapp maintained that he had considered the option of marriage until he learned that Mary had lied and was in fact married to Marcus. He said he was even more upset when he learned that Mary had lied about Marcus being remarried. Knapp asserted that the lies had put a strain on his relationship with Mary.

Knapp had a full proof alibi for the time of Marcus' death; he was with the Vermont National Guard for the week of August 7th through 13th.

What Mary heard is anyone's guess, but Knapp said that on the morning of the 7th, before he went to muster, she had asked him to go shopping for furniture. He told her that there would be plenty of time for picking out furniture when the time was right.

When Knapp got back from his week's military training on Wednesday the 13th, Mary was at the armory to greet him. According to Knapp, Mary told him that she was worried about her husband. Knapp said that Mary reported that she and Marcus had fought the night before. According to Knapp's account, Mary said that Marcus had threatened suicide. There is a question about where Mary and Knapp slept on the night of the 13th; however, it is in the record that on the 14th they shared the same bed. This was the night the body was found and after Mary had witnessed her husband's autopsy.

The Friday that Mary was arrested she wrote Knapp a note. The short message read, "My God, Perham has let it all out. Come quickly and comfort me." It does not appear from the record that Knapp went to the jail.

Although it was fairly clear that Stella Bates knew of the alleged plan, her exact role in the events was questionable. When she was called to testify about the chloroform she said that she had not purchased it; but rather, Leon Perham had bought it at druggist in Hoosick Falls. She would not even admit to knowing how it would be used. Leon had testified that Stella was not at the scene at the time of the murder, giving her one important witness to her innocence.

During the hearing Stella developed another alibi that far exceeded the testimony of Leon. It happened when a married man came forward to tell how he had taken Stella for a walk on the night of Tuesday, July 12th (the night of the murder). The walk extended to Woodford, a distance of six miles. The man and Stella had started out at 7:30 that evening. It appears the couple must have had a lot to talk about as they did not get back until 10:00 the next morning.

At the inquiry it came out that Mary was an optimistic planner even if she lacked skills as a criminal. In the days before Marcus' death, and while Knapp was off with the National Guard, she had visited a furniture store and inquired about purchasing a house full of furniture on credit. Mary told the owner of the store that she was getting married soon and needed the furniture to set up housekeeping. Since she was not employed and would not provide the name of the lucky man, the store owner was hesitant about extending credit. Mary tried to reassure him telling how she would probably be coming by some money soon and would pay off the furniture "in whole."

When he was called to the stand Marcus' brother, William, added yet another twist to the tale. William said that about a month before his death Marcus had come to Bennington in hopes of getting Mary to reconcile. While Marcus was returning to Hoosick by trolley he became violently ill. Marcus was so nauseous that he could not stand the rocking of the trolley. Marcus asked the driver stop while he got off. William said that Marcus had tried to get home by walking along the edge of the track. According to William, Marcus had been so ill he had to spend the night in the brush. When he finally got to William's house on June 15th, Marcus said he suspected he had been poisoned. Marcus remained ill for two more days. On the 18th, Mary, along with three others, had come to the farm in a carriage. Upon seeing Marcus, Mary remarked, "Hello Mark, we came to see if you were living."

The day after Mary's June visit, Marcus and William's father, James, was found dead in his milk wagon. The death occurred on William's farm.

To check the facts of Leon's account, the two deputies took him to the scene of the murder. There he related in detail where and how the entire incident had taken place.

When the hearing concluded, the jury found that Marcus Rogers "came to his death at the hands of his wife, Mary Rogers, Leon Perham and Stella Bates." The three who already in custody would now await a hearing before the grand jury scheduled for the following December.

Justice Shutleff wanted to be sure the three could not contrive a story. He ruled that while they were in jail they could only be visited by their respective attorneys. Stella and Mary were held in the women's portion of the jail briefly, then moved to Rutland which had more space for women prisoners. Leon was kept in Bennington and placed with the other men who were incarcerated.

The Cast of Characters

Mary Rogers was born Mabel Bennett in Hoosick Falls. Throughout her life she had gone by the nickname May; it was later that she added the "r". It was still later that she adopted the name Mary Mabel. She was described as not overly intelligent and some questioned her sanity. At a time when it was believed that insanity was inherited, some attributed her peculiar behaviors to her father, who was considered "strange acting." Her father had to have died when Mary was reasonably young because she had a half-sister less than five years younger than herself.

Mary had neither money enough to dress well nor a natural beauty. She is described as having black hair which accented her alabaster skin. Slim at a time when a Rubenesqué figure was in style, in most ways Mary was rather plain looking. She had, however, developed younger than most girls, which may explain why the record shows that during her short life she had learned some interesting ways of possessing and controlling men. And Mary had thorough control over some men. One of the best examples was that even though Marcus suspected that he had been poisoned in June, less than a month later he went to Bennington in an effort to reconcile with Mary (the very person he suspected of administering the poison). Other examples of her control were seen in her meeting Morris Knapp in June and how by August he was thinking of marrying her. The rumors of Mary's powers went so far as to suggest that she had hypnotized Leon in order to make him a coconspirator. The reality is that she had learned to control by the use of sex. In all probability she had first seduced Boyd in an effort to have him help eliminate Marcus. When she was unable to get Boyd to do her bidding, she seduced young Leon.

Mary was obviously not close to her mother. Mary's mother lived only a few miles from Bennington in Hoosick Falls, yet her mother did not visit Mary for months while she was in jail.

Leon Perham was 19 years old. Like his brother, Boyd, he worked occasionally and still lived at home. A constant smoker, Leon appears from the records to have had limited intellectual capacity. He told the court at the trial that would follow that he could "read and write a bit"; however, on cross-examination he failed to have some rudimentary knowledge.

Nineteen year-old Stella Bates was the more enigmatic character. Born in Kingston, Jamaica, as a child Stella's family had moved to Seattle, Washington. When she was about 14, the Bates family moved to Montreal. By the spring of 1902, when Stella appeared in Bennington, she was not even twenty but had traveled more than most people in the community would in their lifetimes.

Like her friend, Stella also had a way with men. Mary had met Knapp when he took both women for a ride in the country. There was a rumor that Stella had been arrested in Burlington but no record of the arrest was found. The implication was that the arrest was for prostitution.

While she was in Bennington, Stella was not living with her family. Her father and a married sister were living in Troy; a second married sister lived in Cohoes. Unlike Mary who was basically ignored by her family, a few days after Stella's arrest she received a letter from her father. Also unlike Mary who had shown virtually no emotion, while reading her father's letter Stella broke down and cried. It was the first time that she showed any emotion during the events that led to her confinement. The initial weekend Stella was in jail her sister came to visit her; the two siblings had not seen each other in years.

So What Happened

Mary faced two dilemmas. First, she was torn between two men. Emotionally, she was in what she would define as love with Knapp. She believed that Knapp wanted to marry her. Despite the way she treated him, Marcus still wanted her to return so there was no way he would agree to a divorce. There was yet another element; Mary was pregnant and almost certainly not by Marcus.

To solve her problems Mary first tried to get Boyd Perham involved. Boyd was told the intimate details of Mary's plan, which were very similar to the one that was actually executed. She offering him $500 to eliminate Marcus but he refused. She did not give up on Boyd and according to some reports she entered into a "forbidden" relationship with him. In mid-July, Boyd, Mary and Stella had gone for an evening walk. On a bridge upstream from where Marcus would be killed, Mary had asked Boyd to take her to Hoosick. When he asked why she wanted to go there, she told him she wanted to talk to a man (Marcus); she did not give his name. Mary went on to explain that she wanted the man to come to the house; there she would chloroform him and throw him into a brook or river. Mary told how if the man (Marcus) was asleep, he would breathe in the water and then drown. Boyd asked Mary why she wanted the man killed. She said he had an insurance policy and "a little place" that she wanted. According to Boyd, Mary promised that she would give him the $500 from the insurance if he would help. Boyd told her he would help.

A couple of days later, Boyd had a change of heart. He then told Mary he would not do it.

Running out of options, Mary decided to get Leon Perham in a position where he would help her eradicate her problem (Marcus). Out of money and running out of options, she elected to use the one tool that had always worked in the past. Although her dance card was already pretty full, Mary entered into an illicit relationship with Leon.

To put the plan in place Mary needed to get Marcus Rogers to come to Bennington. The problem was she did not want evidence of her invitation. If she wrote a note, Marcus would probably save it, setting the stage for a direct link to her. If she rented a horse and carriage and drove over to extend a personal invitation, the potential existed for a connection to be made. In Mary's resourceful way she resolved the problem by inducing Leon to rent a "rig." He did so under the assumption that he would be taking her to see a man in Hoosick. When Leon brought the horse and carriage to the Perham's house, Mary took it but not him to Hoosick Falls. That was when she invited Marcus to meet her in Bennington. The agreed date was Tuesday, August 12th.

With the date set, the next step was to arrange a scenario that would not raise Marcus' suspicions but would allow her to safely do him in. It was imperative for Mary that Marcus' death look like a suicide. Marcus, a farmer by trade, was naturally strong, so precautions needed to be arranged that would reduce his strength advantage. If her plan worked, she would be free of Marcus, move in with Knapp and just drop Leon like a puppet.

The morning of August 12th, Marcus took the trolley from Hoosick Falls to Bennington. He arrived before 3:00 p.m. and walked over to the porch of the Spaulding house, where Stella lived. This is the house where Mary had lived two months earlier. Mary was sitting with Stella on the porch when Marcus arrived. They took a walk together, stopping on the bridge near where his body would be found two days later. As they parted that afternoon, Mary told him she would meet him later in secluded area next to the river referred to as Morgan's grove. Not all of Marcus' movements that day are known, but it is established that he ate dinner with his aunts'. At 8:00 p.m. he told them he was going out to meet with some friends.

***

Both Mary and Leon appeared calm the evening of the murder. According to their plan, both went to bed around nine o'clock. Leon was so collected that at 9:30 he had actually fallen asleep. An hour later, Mary woke him up saying, "Are you ready to go?" Assuming he would stay awake, Mary left him in his bed so that she could get ready. Leon showed how calm he was by falling back to sleep.

Dressed and ready to go, Mary came back into Leon's room where she sat on his bed while he prepared to go out. This time she had with her a bottle and some handkerchiefs. Noticing Leon's curious look, Mary explained that the bottle contained chloroform that Stella had purchased.

Their alibi was that they were sleeping, so they tried to be as stealth as possible; the two left the house wearing only stockings on their feet. When they went out the back door, Mary propped it very slightly. The door was set to automatically lock and she wanted to be sure they would be able to get back in without anyone noticing. On the rear porch they put on their shoes.

Leon was ready to go and get the deed done. The cooler Mary told him, "Sit down; don't be in a hurry." There, in the quiet of the evening, the two sat for twenty minutes. In a whisper she reviewed the plan one more time. She gave Leon a piece of clothesline she had cut from his mother's backyard to carry in his pocket – it would not do for them to be seen carrying it down the street.

Leaving the house the couple walked two blocks out of their way to the grove by the back entrance. The south end was just down the street but they entered from the north. If by chance anyone saw them enter the grove from the north they would not have been placed at automatically at the scene of the crime. In the dark of the night, Mary and Leon were lost for a few minutes. It was Mary who got them back on the right path.

When they got to the rendezvous Marcus was not there. Patiently, Mary and Leon sat on the rock that protected the bank from fast moving water. They waited for half-an-hour with no sign of Marcus. Finally, Mary got up, walking down the path leading to the street on the south side, far enough that Leon lost sight of her. When she returned, Mary had Marcus with her.

Marcus did not seem concerned that he was not to be alone with Mary. For whatever reason, Marcus took Leon's presence in stride. At Mary's suggestion they sat on the bank. After just a few minutes, Mary said to her husband, "This rock don't sit right, let me have your coat." Marcus stood, removed his jacket and Mary sat on the slight padding. Marcus lay down on the ground placing his head in Mary's lap. The place where they sat down on the bank was the same place where Marcus's body would be pulled out two days later.

In the quiet of the night, the couple engaged in small talk.

Mary asked about his work on the farm; he asked about her health. Little did Marcus know that Mary was pregnant by another man.

When Marcus was relaxed, Mary said, "Stella taught me a new rope trick today." She went on to say, "In this trick anyone can learn to escape."

Mary turned her attention to Leon, instructing him, "Give me the rope." He was all too willing to comply.

She told Marcus to place his hands behind his back. She tied them and in just seconds he was able to escape. She retied them and again he was able to escape. Upping the ante, she suggested that Leon try tying the ropes.

While Leon was putting the final touches on the knots, Mary reached inside the bodice of her dress. When her hand came back out it was carrying the small bottle and a handkerchief. She poured the chloroform onto her handkerchief. The chemical odor was strong and Marcus asked, "What are you doing?"

Mary responded, "Nothing."

Leon, knowing that Marcus was getting wise, finished tying the wrist as fast as he could. Mary tried to hand the handkerchief to Leon but he refused to take it. With her options expiring, Mary took the rag and held it over Marcus' nose and mouth.

Marcus fought back as well as he could; calling out, "Stop!"

Mary told Leon in a very determined tone, "Hold him."

Leon did as he was told and eventually, Marcus stopped struggling enough for Leon to let go. The struggle left Mary so concerned that even when Marcus stopped moving, she refused to take the chloroform away from his mouth and nose.

The plan had called for the unconscious Marcus to be dumped in the water where he would drown in the shallow water. Unfortunately for Mary, he died from the effects of the anesthesia so his lungs would not fill with water and the staged suicide was a failure.

[There is another story about what happened that came out later. In that version, Leon held Marcus and Mary held the handkerchief over Marcus' nose long enough for him to calm down. According to this version, Leon then let go of Marcus and hit him with a small club.]

As she recovered her self control, Mary needed her hands to search Marcus' pockets. She placed the bottle of chloroform on the ground telling Leon, "Take your jackknife out and cut the ropes off his hands." While the bottle was on the ground, the cork fell off; neither of them would notice it was missing that evening. It would be found two days later.

Mary was careful to be sure the pieces of rope were all picked up. In the dark they missed one small piece that, along with the cork, would be found the same day that the body was discovered.

When the ropes were removed from Marcus, Mary told Leon to roll his body down the bank and into the Walloomsac River. As Leon was about to do as he was told, he saw Mary reach into her dead husband's pocket. In the dark, Leon thought he noticed that in her hand she held several pieces of paper. This was probably when she obtained the insurance papers and the missing money. If Leon did not hit Marcus with the club, then it was as Leon rolled the body down the bank that the bruises to the face probably occurred.

The injury over the eye was to cause much suspicion. It was severe enough that at least one doctor would say that he was struck by a blunt instrument. Others would try to pass the injury off as happening as the result of the body's being pushed into the river. During the trial there was never any direct testimony that established that Marcus had been hit by a blunt object.

There would have been a reason for the lack of clarification as to the bruise over the eye. Since Leon was the only one to tell what happened at the river, if he admitted that he hit Marcus it might have raised a question as to the cause of death. If Mary's defense team could raise the speculation that the cause was head trauma, that would have meant that Leon had killed Marcus, not her.

With the body in the river, Mary took her husband's hat and placed the note she had written in advance in the band. She tied the hat to an elm tree, where it would be found the following day.

When the two got home it was approximately 12:30; the

same time that Marcus' watch would stop.

The next morning Mary gave Leon the rope and bottle and told him to hide them. That Friday, after Leon confessed, he took Deputy Nash to the scene, explained what happened, then brought him to his home where he handed over the pieces of rope and the bottle.

Everything matters

While Mary was in jail awaiting her trial, every opportunity to link her name with another story was taken. One Sunday afternoon, Deputy Sheriff Meyers of Washington County, New York took his family for a drive in the country. As they traveled along a rural road, the deputy's wife pointed to a buggy that was ahead of them. When Meyers looked in the direction his wife indicated, he noticed the man jump off the carriage and chase after a woman who had apparently already jumped. When the running man caught up with the woman he hit her several times in the head then grabbed her by the hair and pulled her back toward their wagon.

Meyers pushed his horse faster. As the Meyers' carriage approached the scene, the man was taking the reins of his horse and tying them around the injured woman's neck. The woman was screaming "Murder!" To add to the pandemonium, a four year-old in the wagon was screaming for his father to let go of his mother.

As Meyers' wagon arrived on the scene, the man was heard to say, "Damn you, I'll hang you here and now." Instinctively, Meyers descended from his wagon to intercede on behalf of the wife. Although there was a brief struggle, Meyers easily overpowered the man.

After he was forced to let go of his wife, the man, whose name was Sheehan, told of how they had stopped at a local tavern for a couple of drinks. While they were in the bar, Sheehan said his wife started flirting with another man. Sheehan explained that the reason he was "much excited" was his wife's behavior.

Mrs. Sheehan explained that her husband was jealous but that he "never had no call to be."

It turned out that the Sheehan's had lost a child the year

before. At the funeral the husband had punched his wife and blackened both her eyes.

In covering the story, the newspapers were quick to point out that Mrs. Sheehan's brother was Mary Rogers' stepfather.

Time in Jail

It appears that Vermont was in no hurry to resolve the problem and clearly justice in this case was anything but swift. A grand jury was not scheduled to be convened until the following June (ten months after the murder). Mary, Stella and Leon took up residence jails. Leon's mother and brothers, Boyd and Marshall, would drop by frequently. Stella's father and sisters would come and console her on occasion. Mary had few visitors.

In December 1902, Mary gave birth to a baby that was stillborn; no one (probably not even Mary) was sure who the father was. It was supposed that Mary and Marcus had not slept together since April 1902, which would have meant the baby was full term. Knapp had not met Mary until June of 1902, so that would have made the baby premature. Of course, along the way there was Leon and Boyd. Those are the men who are named, there was probably more. The record is not clear, and not surprisingly, no man claimed to be the parent.

Trial

Mary's trial started in December 1903, sixteen months after the murder. The trial lasted two weeks, ending on December 23rd. The Judge was John H. Watson of Montpelier. The defense team consisted of Daniel Guiltinan of Bennington and Frank Archibald of Manchester. The prosecution was lead by State's Attorney Jacob Shakshober of Arlington, who was assisted by Orin Barber of Bennington.

The state's attorney (frequently called district attorney in other states) had made the decision to have three separate trials. Mary would be first; Leon second and Stella would be tried last. The state's attorney's choice was probably based on the relative strength of the cases. Since Mary had never confessed, the strongest testimony rested in what Leon would say on the stand. If Mary was not convicted, there would be little chance of either of the others being convicted. There was also the element of a plea bargain with Leon. The state's attorney wanted to be sure that Leon would actually testify against Mary before he allowed Leon to plead guilty to murder in the second degree.

At the trial, Leon was the most important prosecution witness. The problem was that Leon was neither intelligent nor sophisticated. Under direct examination, he could be prompted and encouraged. Under the prosecutor's guiding hand, Leon was able to tell his version of the story of what happened on the night of the murder. Leon told the same story he had during the inquest; basically, that it was Mary's idea and all he did was help. He told the jury that he was literally seduced into helping Mary carry out her devious scheme.

Leon's problem, and that of the prosecution, was that his mind could not withstand the rapid volley of cross-examination. His answers either rambled, were unintelligible or he simple did not answer. To demonstrate his lack of credibility, at one point the defense was able to get him to say there were six days in a week, and he had no idea how many inches were in a foot.

The one point the defense was able to raise was that Leon had been told by Boyd that if he told the story he would only be charged with manslaughter and would escape the charge of first degree murder. The defense wanted to be sure the jury knew that Leon stood to gain from his accusations against Mary.

Leon was so weak under cross-examination that the defense would later argue that Mary was "denied" the right to examine her main accuser.

Boyd was called as a witness to tell about having seen Mary and Knapp embrace. On the stand, he also told of the meeting on the bridge where he had at first agreed to help kill Marcus. On cross-examination, the defense tried to show that he was intoxicated at the time of the bridge discussion so he would not remember the details of the discussions. All Boyd would admit to was having "a couple of beers."

Asked why he did not tell the authorities of the plot, Boyd said that he did not think Mary was serious.

At the trial, Mary's acknowledged lover, Morris Knapp, came off less sophisticated than he intended. Regarding his relationship with Mary, he told the same story that he related at the hearing; however, this time he faced cross-examination. Knapp was forced to admit that the very first evening he met Mary and Stella he had proposed that the three go to Schenectady where they would all live together. To the jury, he tried to pass the remark off as a joke. He also admitted that after he moved into the Perham's house in July, he and Mary had spent almost every night together – he could not be made to testify what they did, just that they were together.

Knapp testified that he learned that Mary was married about the middle of July; he said it was the same time that he learned of the insurance. According to Knapp, he "called her down" for the deception that she was single. At the time, adultery was a crime punishable by time in prison. As a result of his Fifth Amendment right, not to have to testify against himself, Knapp could not be forced to explain his physical relationship with Mary after he learned of her marriage. What was clear is that after he did learn she was married, the relationship in all other ways remained close. What is also understood is that the way the Perham's house was laid out, the only way to get to Knapp's bedroom was through Mary's.

It may have part of the defense's strategy to raise reasonable doubt, but the whole courtroom listened when Knapp was asked if he had told Stella that he "had made arrangements to have Rogers put out of the way or killed while you were at muster?" His answer, "No sir, I never did." The point of who planned the murder would be a contention for some time to come.

The prosecution was faced with the problem of how a woman, especially one as slender as Mary, was able to overpower a man as strong as Marcus. Knapp assured those present that Mary was strong – he was probably in the best position to know.

Mrs. Perham was as weak a witness at the trial as she had been at the inquest. She was nervous, often confused and misspoke regularly.

According to Mrs. Perham, when the inquest was taking place Mary had tried to get her and Leon to change their story. Mrs. Perham had told Leon to tell the truth. This was just before he confessed at the inquest.

Mrs. Laura Perham did make two other comments that were minor news. She told of having seen Mary pick Leon up in her arms and carry him across the room – again establishing Mary's strength. Mrs. Perham also told that the only furniture in Mary's room was a mattress resting on a set of springs.

On cross-examination Mrs. Perham broke down and cried. Between her bouts of hysteria, the defense was able to show many discrepancies between her testimony at the trial and what she had testified to at the inquest. The effect these differences had on the jury is questionable.

Marcus' two aunts, Mabel and Myrtle Phillpot, with whom he had spent the evening of the August 12th, each testified. With the exception of making Marcus more human and showing he was loved, they added nothing new until one aunt told of the day after the murder. This aunt told or how Mary came to their house on Wednesday the 13th professing concerns about Marcus. When the aunt said that he probably just went back to his brother's farm, Mary responded that he would not have left without his umbrella and medicine. According to the aunt, no one had mentioned that the medicine was still at her house and the umbrella was hanging under a coat so Mary could not see it. The implication was that Mary had to know before she came to the aunts' house that these items were missing. Obviously, the only way Mary could have known Marcus did not have them was if she had seen him after he left his aunts' home.

Marcus' aunt let out one surprise that was not fully capitalized on by the defense. After he finished supper with her on his last evening, she had said that he should be careful not to take too much of the medicine prescribed by a doctor. Her exact caution was that "it might kill" him. His response: "I wish it would." A comment like this should have been used to bolster the defense's argument that his death was a suicide.

Marcus' brother and employer, William, was called to the stand. The prosecution wanted to impress upon the jury that Mary had some unnamed power over Marcus. The judge was uncomfortable with the line of questioning and the most he would allow William to say was the Marcus would give Mary anything she wanted.

Mary never testified but her demeanor throughout the trial was a statement. With the exception of when Knapp was on the stand, Mary was completely stoic during the trial. She appeared so emotionless that the prosecution would remark about it in its closing argument. Knapp's testimony, however, did cause her to respond. She was tense, giving off the impression that she either felt he was lying or that he had betrayed her. Her expression during his testimony was not that of a lover.

The question of who wrote the note that was found in the hat was addressed by handwriting "experts." The prosecution was able to show that the note was written on paper similar to paper found in the Perham house. It was clear to everyone that the handwriting was not Marcus', which was described as labored; appearing like a "schoolboy's." The writing on the note found in the hat was small and tight, probably belonging to a woman. One witness, a medical doctor, did an unusual comparison. He not only looked at the handwriting; he also compared the spelling. He pointed out that in two other notes used for comparison, Mary had spelled the word anything as enything, any as eny. He went on to show that she misspelled knows as nows and even that Mary was in the habit of not capitalizing the pronoun "i".

The other expert witnesses who testified were a series of doctors. The biggest question concerned whether the bruise above Marcus' eye was severe enough to cause death. The doctors agreed that the injury happened so close to the time of death that they could not be certain if it happened before, after or was the cause. Because Mary had not pleaded "not guilty" by reason of insanity, testimony regarding her sanity was not permitted.

When the prosecution rested, it was 4:30 in the afternoon on a Friday. The judge decided rather than start the defense that late in the day he would close court and the defense would open the following morning.

On Saturday morning there was brief discussion between Mary and her attorney. The attorneys for both sides then approached the bench to confer with the judge. To everyone's surprise, the defense announced it was not going to call any witnesses. The prosecution was instructed to begin its closing arguments. The closing arguments and charge of the jury would take Saturday and most of Monday.

The prosecution's argument was straight forward. They

maintained that Mary planned the murder of her husband in order to get the insurance money and be free to marry Knapp. They focused their argument on the testimony given by Leon, stressing his lack of personal motive. In many ways the prosecution weakened their later case against Leon when they repeatedly referred to him as "Mary's tool."

The defense's closing was more unexpected. In fairness they knew they had to reach to Mary be found not guilty. Not a single witness had shown that Mary was not involved. Not one witness placed her at another location or provided any sort of alibi. The defense's strategy was to paint Knapp as "the blackest scoundrel that ever came upon this witness stand." To them, either Knapp planned the entire scenario or at the very least had significant input. According to the defense, Knapp was even clever enough to give himself an alibi by having the crime committed while he was out of the area. If there was a murder, the defense felt that the failure to charge Knapp was inexcusable.

The defense lawyers even tried to create reasonable doubt by presenting an alternative story. The defense offered the possibility that it was Knapp who induced Leon to murder Marcus; pointing out that it was Knapp who was originally Leon's friend, not Mary. The defense went on to charge that if the case was even as the prosecution believed (Mary wanted the money and Knapp), that the converse would also be true (Knapp wanted Mary and the money). With Marcus out of the way, Knapp would both have Mary and the money.

The defense's last point was that Leon's testimony was given with the assurance that what he said would not be used against him later; in effect he had plea bargained.

It was Judge Watson's first major trial so everyone wondered how he would do in charging the jury. The overall impression was that the Judge had done a good job of defining reasonable cause, and defining the degrees of murder.

Verdict

It had been a long night for the jury. They had finished receiving the judge's charge Monday at 6:30p.m. They had dinner at the hotel then began their deliberations. They immediately agreed to take a vote by paper ballot. When the vote was counted they agreed to go to bed for the night to see if anyone would have a change of heart overnight.

The next morning they took a second vote – the results were the same as on the first ballot. The jury foreman notified the judge that they were ready to proceed. The jury had deliberated for a total of thirty minutes. The courthouse bell was rung and people from throughout the village rushed to get a place in line in hopes of getting a seat in the courtroom. When the doors finally opened, the audience found that the jury was already seated.

At 9:00, Judge Watson entered the room; moments later Mary Rogers was brought in by Sheriff Wilson. There was the trace of a smile on Mary's face until she was told to stand and face the jury. Even now, as the most significant decision about her in her short life was about to be expressed, she stood with an air of arrogance.

The room went silent as the clerk asked the foreman if the jury, which was all men, had reached a verdict. The foreman reached into his pocket and pulled out a crumpled piece of paper. It appeared he was afraid he would say something incorrectly. He read from the paper, "Guilty of murder in the first degree."

Mary's body shook for a moment then she sat back in her chair.

Judge Watson announced that he would render the sentence the following Tuesday. Then as Mary was led from the courtroom by the Sheriff Wilson, the judge called the next case.

Mary was convicted but all the charges related to Marcus' death were not resolved; there was still the fates of Stella and Leon to be settled. Later that afternoon Leon Perham was brought into court. There he stood alone in front of Judge Watson where he pled guilty to murder in the second degree. Like in Mary's case, Watson announced that the sentence would be rendered the following Tuesday.

Stella Bates was then brought before the Judge. The State's Attorney announced that there was not sufficient independent evidence against Stella to warrant a trial. They were unable to find a witness who would testify that it was Stella who purchased the chloroform. Boyd Perham had said she knew of the plan; however, to charge her with prior knowledge would require that they also charge Boyd with the same crime. Since Boyd initially broke the case, to charge him would be counterproductive to future investigations. The State's Attorney recommended that the charges against Stella Bates be dropped and that she be released immediately.

When she was told to pack up her belongings and that she was free to leave, Stella was surprised. She had spent 16 months in jail and suddenly she was free. She told the judge she wanted to leave town and never see it again. The judge agreed and ordered that a train ticket be purchased for her.

With the three cases involving the murder of Marcus Rogers finally resolved, the judge and attorneys had had enough. They packed up their materials and headed to their respective homes; the next day was Christmas Eve.

Stella was taken back to the jail where she packed up her limited belongings, hugged Mary and left the cell. A deputy took Stella to the train station where she was given a ticket to Troy.

For Mary, the release of Stella was the final straw in an emotional day. That morning she had been convicted for first degree murder; that afternoon her coconspirator had been allowed to plea bargain to second degree murder. Now her best friend – maybe her only friend – had been released free of all charges. For the first time since her husband's death, Mary Bennett Rogers became hysterical. She cried, moaned, and pulled at her hair. Her emotions were so strong that the sheriff said she nearly fainted. The woman with the composure of ice was for the first time acting human.

Sentencing

It was December 29th when the sentences were handed down. Like each day of the trial, the courtroom filled to capacity as Mary Rogers and Leon Perham were led in by Sheriff Wilson and Deputy Nash. Like every day of the trial, the number of women in the courtroom exceeded the number of men.

In the fenced in area between the judge's bench and those gathered in the audience, the two convicted murderers were joined by their attorneys as they waited for the judge to enter the chamber. The four appeared to be going over last minute details but in reality everyone knew what was would be heard from the judge. The only sentence for murder in the first degree was death by hanging. The only sentence for murder in the second degree was life in prison. It was the pair's reactions that those who gathered in the crowded courtroom wanted to witness.

Perham's paler could not be missed as he rose first to hear the judge issue his fate. When the judge pronounced that he would serve a life sentence at hard labor, Perham turned looked and out the window. It was as if he expected the light to give him the strength to withstand the decree. Without saying a single word, Leon Perham, age 20, returned to his seat. Some of those in the audience expected that because he had cooperated with the prosecution and because of his personal intellectual limitations, his sentence would be reduced. A shorter sentence was not an option for the judge.

Everyone in attendance's eyes had been fixed on Mary from the moment she entered the room. Would the cool, heartless killer show emotion for only the third time in the trial? [When Knapp testified, she had shown some emotion and there was a momentary glimpse when the verdict was announced.]

Mary was told to stand. The judge asked if there were any reasons why the sentence should not be imposed. She lifted her hands one at a time to her temples; she silently rubbed as if the act might send the dream away. Finally, Mary responded at a level just over that of a whisper, "I'm not guilty." The words were said so softly that only those in the front rows could hear what she had said.

She had spoken; that was all the Judge Watson needed. He sentenced her to be hung on the first Friday in February, 1905. The reason for the year delay was a matter of Vermont statute. At this time, the governor of Vermont could not issue a pardon; pardons were the exclusive domain of the legislature. By law, no executions could be conducted until the legislature had had the opportunity to meet. The legislature only met every other year with the next session scheduled for fall 1904. This set of laws meant that the earliest Mary would face the ultimate punishment was the date given by the judge.

In the meantime, Judge Watson assigned Mary to hard

labor at the prison in Windsor. The judge said that the hard labor was to end three months before the hanging. The final months of her stay she was to be in solitary confinement.

Like Leon, Mary had looked out the window as the judge spoke. The only emotion she had shown were the brief moments when she was nearly speechless.

With the verdict in, the natural assumption would be that the sentence would be in accordance with the crime. The problem was that even in 1903, Vermonters opposed the death penalty. The last person put to death was in 1892. Every person convicted of murder in Vermont after 1892 had had his or her sentence commuted to life in prison by the legislature. In the 25 cases of murder in Bennington County, only one had resulted in the person suffering the death penalty and that case was in 1832.

Windsor prison was for both women and men. Vermont at the time did not have a separate prison for women.

"The truth has not been told."

"If it should be it would open peoples eyes in Bennington and I should not be going to Windsor with a rope hanging over me."

A reporter from the Bennington newspaper was permitted to interview Mary in her cell in the days before she was taken to Windsor Prison. During their discussion, Mary expressed her feelings that the trial had not been "well handled"; a direct charge against her court appointed lawyers. She went on to say that she never planned to kill her husband, implying the plan was made by someone else. Mary went so far as to infer that the person was an accomplice and further that the people of Bennington would not be happy if they knew the whole story, saying: "The one who laid the plans and schemed the most in the matter would not be walking the streets a free man." Everyone in town knew, without her saying so, that the person Mary felt held more guilt was Morris Knapp.

Told that Knapp had recently married, Mary became incensed. She started calling everyone from the Phillpots to Marcus' brother William, liars. She then let her anger loose on Leon saying that he told "a pack of lies." It was, however, for Knapp that she let loose her greatest venom. She accused him of lying from the beginning. According to Mary, Knapp knew from the night they met that she was a married woman. She said that he "teased me into things I never thought of until he suggested them." As she cooled down, Mary added rather philosophically, "If I should say the truth, everybody would say I was lying, too."

Asked directly if she had killed Marcus, Mary responded, "I am convicted of killing him and whatever I may say now would do no good."

The reporter described Mary as "stupid" and "ignorant" saying that her "stupidity had been mistaken for nerve." He may have been right; however, the logic and synthesis he ascribes to her make her appear to be more unsophisticated and a product of her environment than in any way intellectually limited.

Following the sentencing, Mary was visited by her mother. During the meeting Mary broke down in tears. Part of her despair was attributed to not hearing from Stella. After her mother left, Mary realized that she was truly alone; there were intermittent tears all afternoon.

Within two days of their sentencing both Mary and Leon were on their way to the State penitentiary at Windsor. For both it was to supposed to be a one way trip.

Mary Rogers may have left town but her story was far from over.

Mary had shown herself to be resourceful even though she was without resources. She had been defiant even though she had virtually no defense. She traded her body for things she could not otherwise afford. She was convicted of a murder supposedly for love; yet, she had demonstrated virtually no emotion at her trial. Although men became entrapped in her web, ultimately they would all turn against her. If she had done anything, Mary Bennett Rogers had proven she was difficult to grasp.

What next?

For the people of Bennington, one would have assumed it was time to get back to some form of normalcy. After all, Stella had effectively been banished from the village; Mary and Leon were convicted and shipped off to Windsor. It was winter, Christmas was over, the open houses associated with New Years Day were about to happen, perhaps people would finally find something else to talk about besides a year-old murder.

There was, however, one thing that would hold the community back from the calm it so dearly desired. There was about to be a second murder trial. In this new trial the defendant was also a woman. Again, there had been an attack on a husband. Like Mary Rogers, the alleged motive was the love of another man. Unlike Mary, Alice Moffatt's husband did not die as the result of the poison he ingested. The cases were too similar to be ignored while being exceptionally different; in Mrs. Moffatt's case, bail had been put forward by her husband, while all of Mary's friends had been in jail with her. [This story will be in the next book **The Ladies are Back**.]

Next

It is difficult to determine another person's motives; however, that does never stop us from trying. Exactly why Mary's attorney, Frank Archibald, waived the exceptions he had taken during the trial may never be known, but by doing so he weakened her chance of gaining an appeal. There is a strong prospect that Archibald's reasoning was a long standing record Vermont had in dealing with people facing the death penalty. Archibald was in a position to know the practice, since in addition to being Mary's attorney he was a State Assemblyman. It had been eleven years since Vermont had executed anyone. That record was not because Vermont was free of violent crime; there had been several people sentenced to death in the intervening years. What the record means is that each time a person was convicted of first degree murder, the legislature had commuted the sentence from death to life in prison. Archibald undoubtedly assumed that the legislature would act as it always had when, in October of 1904, he introduced legislation to commute Mary's sentence.

When Mary was interviewed in Bennington before being taken to Windsor Prison, she said she was slightly apprehensive about the legislature acting on her behalf. Most would have thought she had little to worry about. In 1883, Mrs. Isabella Meaker became the only other woman ever hung in Vermont. To add to Mary's security, Mrs. Meaker's crime was much more repulsive. At 42, Mrs. Meaker had taken in her husband's orphaned eight year-old half-sister Alice. For her generosity Mrs. Meaker received a lump sum payment of $400 to raise the child. After a year of having precocious Alice in the house, Mrs. Meaker decided to decrease her expenses. She sent her son to buy $.10 worth of strychnine and rent a carriage. Mrs. Meaker poisoned Alice, while her son drove the carriage toward a place where they planned to dispose of the young girl's body. After giving Alice the poison, Mrs. Meaker went so far as to hold her hand over the child's mouth to keep her from screaming. Alice died sooner than they expected and fearing they would be seen with the body of a child in the carriage, they left Alice's limp body in a swamp. The nature of Mrs. Meaker's crime was so repulsive that the legislature did not commute her sentence.

In contrast, in 1898, Mrs. Isabella Marsh and her lover were convicted of poisoning Mr. Marsh. The motive was so the two lovers could be together. Both of Mrs. Marsh and her lover's sentences were commuted to life in prison by the legislature. Comparing the crimes, it would seem that Mary's crime was more in line with Mrs. Marsh's than Mrs. Meaker's.

Whatever the combination of reasons, the 1904 Vermont Legislature was not leaning toward clemency. The act to commute Mary's sentences was debated but ultimately it lost by almost 40 votes. Since the legislature only met every other year, that late October vote meant that Mary, who was scheduled to be hung in February of 1905, would be executed before the legislature would meet again in 1906.

From the beginning there had always been something different about Mary and her case and the situation before the legislature is just one more example of those differences.

With action by the legislature no longer an option, the only way to save Mary's life was to start the process of legal appeals. Although Archibald would initiate the appeal, he would be replaced by two lawyers not involved in her original trial. Mary's new lawyers were Charles A. McCarthy of Hoosick Falls and Thomas Moloney of Rutland. These two would later be joined by John Senter, the former United States Attorney for Vermont.

Appeal, Politics, a Cause & Scandal

Mary was less than an ideal prisoner. Over the year she was in Windsor she was assigned to the prison laundry and to the kitchen. In both places she had to be sent back to her cell for talking too much to the other women assigned to the same stations and for her belligerence. Although the female matron, Miss Durkee, appeared to hold a hard line with regard to Mary, later events would cast the matron in a different light.

As her February 3rd date with destiny approached, Mary met regularly with the priest assigned to the prison and she was again baptized into the Roman Catholic Church.

There was an interesting story carried in a St. Albans' newspaper. The reporter had learned that while Mary worked in the kitchen, she would have been able to walk out an unlocked door that led into a vestibule at the front of the prison. From there she could have crossed the open lawn of the prison. It would seem that for months Mary had been in a position where the turning of one handle would have resulted in freedom.

There is no way to know if Mary knew of the unlocked door or not, but throughout her ordeals, Mary had never fled.

Appeal

From the time the appeal began until the scheduled execution was only three months. Mary's attorney's immediately tried to find evidence that had been missed, overlooked, or ignored at the time of the trial and what was called "errors" made in the original trial.

The judge in Mary's trial had included in her sentence that, three months before her execution, she was to be moved into solitary confinement. This would be a time for her to reflect on her acts and come to terms with her fate. Within days of the legislature's vote, Mary was moved from her cell to a block of cells reserved for those waiting to die or unable to exist within the general population of the prison.

The first new evidence Mary's attorneys were able to obtain was a confession by Leon Perham that he was the person who killed Marcus. Perham's confession stated that he hit Marcus in the head with a club.

If Perham's confession was true, it would explain two facts; the bruise over Marcus's eye and why there were no burn marks on his face. If chloroform is left on a person's face too long the active ingredients cause burns on the skin. At Mary's trial, Perham had testified that Mary held the handkerchief over Marcus' mouth and nose for fifteen to twenty minutes. Exposure for that period of time to the quantity of chloroform the prosecution said was used should have caused burns.

Other evidence that was "discovered" was a history of insanity in Mary's family. Most of the insanity was in Mary's father's family [Mary's father was dead and could not defend his sanity]. According to the accounts, some members of her paternal side had been committed to asylums. The defense team was also able to get statements from some of Mary's neighbors when she was a child. These statements said that Mary had a history of acting "strange."

Mary's lawyers were also able to get statements from two doctors relating to Mary's behavior. One of the more unusual statements they were able to obtain was from the doctor Mary visited in days before Marcus' murder. According to the doctor, when Mary found out she was pregnant, she acted insane demanding that he perform an abortion. There was also a statement from the doctor who was present when Mary had the stillborn birth in the jail in Rutland (she and Stella had been moved while they waited for their trials). According to this doctor, during the birth Mary acted like an insane person.

The lawyers also had concern, stated in the newspaper but not followed up on in the court documents, about whether the jury had religious bias. Mary was Catholic.

A new Governor

In 1904 the people of Vermont elected as Governor Civil War veteran, Charles Bell. Along with the traditional duties of his office, Bell inherited Mary and her sentence.

Bell soon learned that just because the Governor of Vermont was not permitted commute the sentence of a person convicted of murder in the first degree, does not mean that he was without some authority concerning Mary's fate. Under the law, Bell had the authority to postpone her execution.

Shortly after he took office, Mary wrote Governor Bell a

letter asking to meet with him to discuss a reprieve changing the date of her execution. When he was asked about Mary's writing, the Governor responded that the letter was wonderful and above his expectations of her abilities. On January 19, 1905, approximately two weeks before her scheduled execution, Governor Bell met with Mary. He was quoted as saying as he was leaving her cell: "I wish I could save her."

Mary and the Media

When the legislature failed to commute Mary's sentence, Mary's story was recharged in the press. By allowing a woman to be scheduled for hanging, Vermont was not doing well in the national press. The issues in Mary's case were part of a national debate about the suitability of the death penalty. One side holding that the death penalty was justice and the other holding it was a remnant of our country's barbaric past. There was a second issue of the suitability of hanging. If during a hanging the person's neck did not break, he or she suffered several minutes of strangulation. On occasion, and especially with women, the head would literally be ripped from the body, a most unpleasant outcome. The debate about hanging set the stage where any incidents in Mary's story sold newspapers.

The cell Mary was assigned for her last three months overlooked the front lawns of the prison. Representatives of the newspapers were constantly asking for permission to interview and photograph Mary. They were all denied access. Little did the media seem to realize that the woman looking out of the prison window at them was the same woman that they so desperately wanted to photograph.

There was a serious question as to who would be allowed to attend the execution. There were times when the general public had been allowed to attend a hanging. The newspapers even carried stories told by some of Vermont's senior citizens about how, when they were young, they had attended the hangings. One woman told how she walked 40 miles to see the man hang, fearing she would never again have a chance to witness such an occurrence (She had assumed correctly).

Vermont law did not restrict the number who could attend an execution, but did require that at least 12 people be witnesses.

To close out their stories of Mary Rogers, the various newspapers all wanted to have a representative present when the trapdoor was sprung. The out-of-state news reports about Mary had already had a toxic effect on the state, so there was little desire by the state officials to make her death a spectacle. The question became: should members of the press be admitted and, if so, how would they be selected?

The movement

"When I return, I expect to have ready for publication one of the most piteous and astounding stories of recent times. Access has been given to me to things no newspaper would find it possible to uncover. When my statement has been made it may be the state of Vermont will require no further appeal to its right mindedness. I am now working to avert a blot upon the history of my country." With those words Mrs. Cecilia Blickensderfer left Stamford, Connecticut for Vermont in support of her newest cause – the life of Mary Rogers.

Mrs. Blickensderfer was wealthy; her husband, William, was the Vice President and Treasurer of Blickensderfer Typewriter Company. At that time, the company was the leader in the manufacture of portable typewriters. With no children of her own, Cecilia had become recognized for her humanitarian efforts; her husband was renowned as a naturalist. Known for taking the side of women in trouble, Cecilia became involved in Mary's case. It does not appear that Cecilia felt that Mary was innocent so much as that death by hanging was inappropriate.

Mrs. Blickensderfer's involvement altered the playing field. Cecilia's well recognized name facilitated the ability to get Mary's cause covered by the newspapers. In the months that would follow, Mrs. Blickensderfer spoke before women's groups throughout the northeast in an effort to raise enough money to take Mary's appeal to the Supreme Court of the United States if necessary.

In late January 1905, Cecilia went to Bennington County where in a 24 hour period she was able to obtain the signature of six of the jurors in Mary's trial asking that her sentence be commuted. The reason they had changed their opinion was the confession by Leon in which he admitted to having struck Marcus with a club.

With the signatures of six jurors and with petitions carrying the signatures of thousands of other men and women in hand, Cecilia Blickensderfer descended on Montpelier, bent on having Governor Bell postpone the execution.

A scandal begins

A few days before Mary's execution, an unnamed person from Boston mailed an envelope containing $250 in cash to a guard at Windsor Prison. The note that accompanied the cash asked the guard to purchase some poison so that Mary might commit suicide. The letter, which was not signed, assured the guard that when she was dispelled of, he would be sent a like amount.

The guard who received the cash was named Harpin. Harpin allegedly turned the money over to the warden of the prison who just happened to be his father. Warden Harpin shared the news with the superintendent of the prisons, Oakes, and he with Governor Bell. With this many people knowing of the incident it was just a matter of time before the media would find out.

Law enforcement is heard from

There was an interesting quirk in Vermont law regarding the execution of prisoners. The actual hanging of a prisoner was to be conducted by the Sheriff of the county in which the prison was built, not by the warden of the prison. In Mary's case, this law meant that the Sheriff H. H. Peck of Windsor County was required to pull the trapdoor and his deputies were to provide whatever support was required.

During the year Mary had been housed in Windsor Prison, Peck and his deputies had never met Mary, but because of the uproar she caused they had come to know her circumstances. In the days just before February 2nd, Peck and four of his deputies wrote a letter, some would call it a petition, to Governor Bell asking that he stay her execution. The officers noted that Leon Perham had recently changed his story and now claimed that he was the primary perpetrator in the murder of Marcus Rogers. The officers also called into question Mary's sanity at the time, citing her pregnancy and the history of insanity in her family.

The politics of the time and the sentiment concerning capital punishment expressed in the letter written by the men who were to conduct the hanging requires that a portion be included.

> "We understand our duty and will all shall endeavor to do our duty as officers under the law, but though we are officers we cannot forget that we are men – men with homes – citizens of Vermont, whose good repute is dear to us all.
>
> We, therefore, present this petition moved only by the ambition to render the State our highest and best service with an abiding faith that in time to come it will be abundantly demonstrated that we have performed a higher duty to the law, to order, and to civilization that if not compelled to hang this woman by the neck until dead."

Upon receiving the letter from Sheriff Peck and his deputies, Governor Bell took a hard line indicating that if the men did not want to do their duty they were free to resign. He would characterize the Sheriff's actions as "unprecedented and out of place."

A rumor started that the Sheriff and his deputies would resign minutes before the execution, thus making the appointed time pass without the required officers and automatically granting Mary a reprieve. Bell assured the people of Vermont that if the Sheriff did resign, he would have officers ready who would conduct the execution of Mary. The legality of the governor's assertion might have been a very real question because the Sheriff is an elected position and the law said that the sheriff of the county in question was the one charged with carrying out the execution, not a substitute.

Time runs out

The problem for Mary's new defense team was that the three months had not been enough time to organize and present the information for an appeal to the Vermont Supreme Court. They had Leon's confession, statements from the doctors and neighbors about the possibility of insanity; however, they were running out of time. In a play reminiscent of lawyers today, they took their case to the media, claiming Mary's death under the circumstances would be unfair.

In the last days of January and the first days of February, Mary was confined to her cell. She sat there listening to the pounding of hammers. She repeatedly asked those charged with watching her, "Are those for me?" Although never answered, she knew they were.

On Thursday, February 2nd, after the priest had administered last rites, Governor Bell sent a message to the warden at Windsor Prison postponing Mary's execution from February 3 to June 2. The new date was chosen to allow her case to be heard in the May term of Vermont's Supreme Court. Bell assumed that he was allowing her attorneys time to prepare and submit her appeal. By the time Mary received the word of the reprieve, the scaffold had already been built. Mary's remark when Sheriff Peck delivered the news of the extension on her life was that Governor Bell was "a good man."

The message of her temporary stay had been delivered by Sheriff Peck. This was the first time the two had met. Peck was struck by how Mary expressed no emotions at the news. She had been writing a letter to her mother when he came to the floor and upon hearing the news she returned to her writing.

To avoid speculation as to the reasons he granted a reprieve, Governor Bell released a press statement. His reasoning in his own words: "I do this expressly and only on the ground that she claims, through her attorney, that she had not been given a fair trial and that the evidence presented against her was false." He went on to say, "I do not in any way pass upon the question as to whether such was the fact. I leave that question to the court, to which she now has full recourse."

Bell went on to express his views on the entire matter. He started by saying that in no way was he influenced by outsiders who felt the Vermont's laws were "cruel and barbaric." [Terms used in editorials and speeches on the sentence.] He also said that he had no intention of proposing legislation that would end capital punishment. After saying he would pass on the question of facts, Bell added in an interview that he put no stock in Leon's confession, going so far as to call Perham a liar (meaning in his prison statement).

Bell made his position on future reprieves very clear. He said that in his opinion it was the duty of the governor "to execute, not defy the expressed will of the courts." Going on to say that he would not be moved by "prejudice or passion, and (all further decision would be) in according to my interpretation of justice, the laws of the state and my own conscience." In short, if Mary failed in the courts, she would be granted no further help from the governor.

Mary's story was now supposed to go into remission, at least until May; however, that was not what happened.

Scandal Part II

By early March 1905, one of Vermont's leading newspapers, *The Rutland Herald,* printed a story about an investigation it was conducting of the state's prisons. The newspaper's examination was specifically focused on Windsor Prison, the one where Mary was housed. As the *Herald's* investigation continued, more and more newspapers joined in. The coverage of the scandal makes interesting reading in almost all the Vermont newspapers in the fall of 1905.

The *Herald's* investigation was brought on by a series of events. One was the release of the information about the guard receiving cash for poison. The newspaper learned that subsequent to the money arriving, both of the Harpins, father and son, were dismissed by Superintendent Oakes. The question became why?

A small part of what the *Herald* was trying to discover is if there was any truth to the rumor that Mary was in a "delicate" condition. Everyone knew she had been pregnant and not sure of the baby's father when she was originally arrested, but under the watchful eye of the guards there is no way she should be "in a family way" now. The newspaper wanted to know how such a story could have started.

One of the first problems the *Herald* encountered was the hard, silent line drawn regarding incidents inside the prison. Said politely, what happened within the prison's walls stayed within the walls. The new warden of Windsor Prison, C. S. Palmer, who replaced Harpin, wanted to dispel the rumor about Mary. In an unusual break of policy, the newspaper was able to interview the prison's matron, Miss Durkee, who assured the reporter that there was no truth to the allegation.

As the *Herald's* investigation began to make some discoveries regarding graft, possible corruption, and issues within the prison population, Superintendent Oakes became anxious. He was advised by his doctor that he should resign for health reasons.

Oakes had dismissed the Harpins then resigned himself, setting the stage for the newspaper's dream. There were suddenly two sides, those who supported Oakes and those who supported the Harpins. Now the silent wall would break down and stories would become prevalent. Since everyone involved had taken sides, what came out was colored by perception as much as truth.

In May of 1905, Oakes was replaced as Superintendent of the prisons by William Lovell. Shortly after starting in his new position, Lovell noticed a couple of prisoners acting strangely. He ordered them to be taken to a holding room until the prison's doctor could arrive. The doctor established that they were under the influence of morphine. The prisoners in question were not under the care of a physician, so the issue became where did they get the drug? The superintendent began an investigation that would lead to a scandal. The scandal would eventually involve multiple guards and would destroy the reputation of Oakes, the former prison superintendent. The scandal would do little for the state of Vermont, which was already trying to end the situation with Mary.

The prisoner under the influence provided the name of the guard who had smuggled the morphine into the prison. The guard immediately disappeared but was soon found in Boston. He was arrested and returned to Vermont to face criminal charges. Fearing flight again, he would not be allowed to be released on bail. It would turn out that there was a practice of supplying drugs to prisoners in exchange for items belonging to the prison.

One of the primary businesses of Windsor Prison was the manufacturing of shoes. Leon Perham, Mary's accomplice, was serving his hard labor in the prison's shoe factory. During the investigation it came out that two other guards brought in food which they traded for pairs of heels. Both of these guards were arrested but were released on bail pending the result of their hearings.

As the activities between the guards and the prisoners became exposed, so did some activities between guards and employees of the prison. It was soon learned that the wife of a former guard named Burr had a suit against one Miss Kimball, one of the women employed in the prison. Mrs. Burr was suiting for alienation of affection. In simple English, the husband and the employee were having an affair inside the prison walls. One of was issues confronting Mrs. Burr was that her three best witnesses in the alienation suit were the same three guards that had been arrested for supplying drugs or food to prisoners.

What was first discovered about the guards was not all of that would be uncovered. With her personality and behavioral pattern, Mary Rogers was not to be left out of a good scandal.

The Vermont Supreme Court

The Supreme Court of Vermont consisted of seven members. It took two justices to agree that an appeal had merit for the full panel to hear arguments. There was a long, bitter debate as to whether the court would even hear Mary's appeal. Although the decision to allow a hearing before the Court should be on the merits of the appeal, one can not rule out the issue of how Vermont was appearing in the media. The problem of Mary's case was exacerbated by the ongoing scandal in the prison. Finally, on April 29th, the chief justice and the most senior justice agreed that the full court would hear Mary's appeal on May 17th.

The seven judges listened to the arguments, including the admission of evidence where the new warden Lovell stated he was present when Leon Perham said he lied in the initial trial to save his own life. By a vote of five to two, the Vermont Supreme Court held that there was not enough new evidence to warrant a new trial. The majority opinion was written by Justice John Watson, the same person who had presided at Mary's trial. Today, if a judge decides at one level, he or she is expected to recluse him or herself from an appeal; not so, Judge Watson actually wrote a 40 page opinion basically holding that any evidence that had been discovered was not sufficient to have changed the guilty verdict. Note: Mrs. Blickensderfer had already secured the signature of six of the original jurors saying they would have not found Mary guilty of first degree murder had they seen the evidence.

The decision of the Vermont Supreme Court came down just days before Mary's stay was to run out. Like in January, Mary had been placed in solitary confinement and the gallows were constructed in anticipation of an adverse verdict. As soon as the decision was rendered, Mary's attorneys announced that they intended to take her case to the United States Supreme Court. Based on their appeal, Governor Bell was trapped. There was not time enough for the defense to apply to the Supreme Court before the scheduled execution on June 2nd. Bell granted yet one more reprieve to Mary rescheduling the execution for June 23, the last date the United States Supreme Court would be in session.

Mary's lawyers did the best they could to try to get an appeal before the US Supreme Court in the three weeks they were given. As it became apparent that they would not succeed in having word from the court before June 23rd, Bell was boxed in one more time. Governor Bell, in an effort to assure that Mary had every opportunity for appeal, stayed her execution for a third time. With this delay, the date of December 8, 1905 was selected for her hanging.

When Sheriff Peck brought Mary the news of the further reprieve she was naturally relieved. She had been sitting in her cell for days listening once again to sounds of hammers in courtyard below. In response to the news, Mary called Governor Bell "a great good man."

While Sheriff Peck was with Mary he received a surprise. Mary had made the sheriff a simple gift, which she gave him in a small packet. Later, when he opened the present, he found a note and a small booklet. The note read:

"Mr. Peck – Please do no think me precipitate in asking you to accept such a very simple gift as this little book. I am no drawer by any means, and it is probable that you will find many mistakes within. I have made a number of such little books for some friends as a token of rememberance [sic], and at last decided I would make you one, for I feel that you are a friend indeed. I feel greatly indebted to you for what you have done for me, Mr. Peck, and to many others. May God bless you.

Mabel."

The book was simple collection of Mary's thoughts during her stay in solitary confinement.

The Supreme Court - US

In late June 1905, it was decided that the Supreme Court would hear arguments in the case of Mary Rogers. The next problem became when. The Governor's stay was only until December 8th and the court, much as today, took its time in making decisions.

On October 9th, the Supreme Court heard arguments by both Fitts, the Attorney General of Vermont, and Mary's attorney, Thomas Moloney, contending that if the Supreme Court did not act then the Governor would allow Mary's execution on the appointed day. To some it might appear that there was an attempt being made by the Governor to hold the Supreme Court hostage.

October 16th, the Supreme Court relented and scheduled arguments in Mary's case for November 6th. In doing so the Supreme Court went on to say that now the matter (fate of Mary) was in their hands, adding that the State had no authority to act on Mary's execution until they (the members of the Supreme Court) had ruled. By the courts decision, responsibility for Mary's confinement was officially assigned to a Federal Marshal. In reality nothing changed as Mary remained in the same cell as before. The effect of the ruling was that there was now a standoff between the authority of the State and that of the United States Supreme Court.

The Scandal Part III

By the fall of 1905, the situation in the prisons had drawn enough attention that the state appointed a special commission to investigate what had occurred. The commission was comprised of three men. That fall, they held hearings that were open to the public, which included the media. The reports of this investigation were carried by newspapers throughout the state and even the *New York Times*. Reports about the investigation were as compelling to the people of the Vermont as any scandal today.

There were several other incidents brought forward, some proven, some suggested. One unsubstantiated story was that a prisoner was allowed to escape by posing as dead. He was allegedly taken out of the prison by the undertaker. When called before a commission assigned to investigate the scandal, the undertaker insisted the man was in fact dead and had been embalmed at the prison. There was a second story involving a Mrs. Barry, the wife of a prisoner convicted of larceny. She took a position working in Warden Harpin's home. According to the testimony, the woman and the warden became intimate. When the prisoner found out about his wife's behavior, he wanted a divorce. Unable to find witnesses willing to testify in a divorce suit, the prisoner confessed to the crime for which he had already been convicted; however, in his confession he claimed that his wife had been an accessory to the crime. Suddenly, Mrs. Barry went from maid to a suspect in a crime. Harpin quickly got the Mrs. Barry out of town.

It would take until the investigation in fall of 1905 for the full extent of Mary's segment in the scandal to become public knowledge. Like every other part of Mary's story, her role in the scandal would garner public interest.

One of the prison trustees, Vernon Rogers (no relation), was assigned to clean the floors in the women's section of the prison. It was well established practice at Windsor Prison that any contact between male and female prisoners was prohibited. When Vernon received the assignment in the women's section, at least one of the guards had joked with him about how much fun he could have if he was able to go into Mary's cell.

While Vernon was sweeping the floor outside Mary's cell, he heard a gentle knocking from inside her door. The knocking was followed by a soft voice. Even though it was against the prison policy, Vernon began conversing with Mary through the door. As time went on, they began speaking almost every time he cleaned. During their discussions Vernon told Mary he was depressed over being in prison. Mary assured him that she understood his feelings and "wished he would come in" (her cell). Vernon assured Mary that he "wished he was" (inside). As time went by, Mary asked if there was any way he could get a key.

The idea of Mary's company must have intrigued Vernon because he set about trying to figure a way in to her cell. First, he learned from one of the guards that her lock was so old that "any old key would work." The problem for Vernon was that he had no idea how to make a key. The issue was resolved when Vernon propositioned one of the other prisoners to make him a skeleton key in the prison's shop. The second problem was that the key the fellow prisoner made was too short and would not unlock the inner portion of the lock. It was Mary's turn to help.

Mary asked the warden for a pair of scissors so that she could cut out patterns. At first she was told "no." The warden at the time was Harpin. He approved Mary having scissors when a guard found a pair with rounded ends. The rounded ends proved to be just what Mary needed. She used them as a screwdriver removing the plate on the inside of her cell lock. Over the course of the next several months, Vernon and Mary kept company in her cell several times. On more than one occasion, Mary and Vernon were alone in her cell as the scaffold was being constructed in the courtyard outside her window.

The questions for the commission became why was Mary allowed scissors and second, who provided the scissors? In both cases, the preliminary answers in the newspapers were one name, two people. The Harpins, father and son respectively, were believed to have Ok'd and provided the scissors. Months later it would come out that permission for the scissors came from the superintendent Oakes, not the warden (Harpin) of the prison and that the scissors had come from another guard. The Harpins were cleared on this set of charges.

Mary's antics were far from over with Vernon. As the scandal was breaking, people employed by the prison either resigned or were dismissed. By March 1905, the prison suddenly had several openings for staff positions, including one in the women's division. Miss Durkee, the head matron of the prison, seemed to have been coming off as one of the good-guys in the newspaper stories. To help fill the staffing voids, Durkee suggested that her niece, a Miss Kimball, should be hired as a female assistant. At first, Warden Lovell questioned the decision, but assured of the girl's character by Miss Durkee, he relented and the niece was hired.

Kimball, being new, was assigned to the night shift. While the scandal was being investigated, Kimball, unwisely, began the practice of taking Mary out of her assigned cell at night. Mary was then walked to Kimball's own space which had a comfortable bed. Kimball's space adjoined the male guards lounge. According to at least one report, while in Kimball's room Mary was visited by the male guards. Miss Kimball's behavior was not discovered until late October near the end of the prison investigation.

For her conduct Kimball was dismissed – it appears that some of the guards in question were the same ones who had been bringing food and drugs to the prisoners (these men had already been dismissed).

It is worthy of note that Kimball was only sixteen at the time and, on a personal note, was the same woman charged with alienation of affections in the Burr's marriage.

November 1905

In a two day period, Mary's behaviors were scheduled to be considered in two very different venues. On November 6th the Supreme Court was to hear her appeal; Mary was not to be present. On November 7th Mary was expected to testify before the commission examining Windsor Prison.

Mary's attorney argued her case before the Supreme Court. One of her attorneys, John Sentor, had previously been the Federal Attorney for Vermont. Young State Attorney General Clarke Fitts represented the State of Vermont.

Those readers who had been following the prison scandal and were expecting to be able to read Mary's side of the details of her behavior in the prison were to be disappointed. Since the commission's hearing had been open to the media, the members of the commission chose to meet with her in private rather than create a public spectacle. Mary's side of the allegations was never directly reported. Other than letters that were not approved that were snuck out of the prison, we do not know why Mary allowed the guards to visit her.

Naturally, the question in November of 1905 became, was Mary again in a "family way"? With her not appearing before the commission, the explanation was that she was and they did not want to members of the media to see her. The prison doctor was brought in. He released a statement to assure the people of the state that Mary Rogers was not pregnant.

During the course of the legal appeal between letters and

petitions, Governor Bell had received over 40,000 signatures from people asking that Mary's sentence be commuted to life in prison. But not all the letters went to the Governor; Cecilia Blickensderfer had received some of her own. The letters Cecilia received fell into two categories. Some supported her and her efforts on Mary's behalf. Others were abusive.

The Supreme Court Decides

On November 27th the Supreme Court ruled. By deciding so quickly, the justices avoided a potentially dangerous standoff with the State of Vermont. The judges ruled that there were no errors in Mary's original trial or in the way her case was handled on appeal. With ten days to go, Mary's fate was decided.

It was reported that when Mary heard of the Supreme Court's decision she openly wept. If that was the case, it was only the second time since she was incarcerated thirty nine months before that her emotions took control (the other time was when Stella was released).

Fate

With the United States Supreme Court ruling the last legal hope was over. Governor Bell had made his position clear; he would not postpone the execution if all the legal avenues were exhausted. Mary was out of options. The hanging was scheduled for December 8, 1905 between the hours of one and two in the afternoon. There were those who were concerned that the one hour time limit was too restrictive. Their apprehension was, what would happen if the scaffold was not finished in time or there was a problem with either the rope or trapdoor. There would not be time to fix the problem since there was a specific ending time of 2:00. If any of those glitches were to occur, Mary would once again avoid her fate.

Mary was placed once again on what was called a death watch. This was the third time Mary had been on the death watch. As a result of the prison scandal, a couple named Loukes from near Burlington was brought in to supervise every movement made by Mary. This time she would not be under the care of Miss Durkee. Before going into her last cell, Mary was stripped, searched, and even provided with a new set of clothes. Additionally, her cell had all new furniture, which had been searched for contraband or for any objects she could use to hurt herself. A guard or a member of the family assigned to watch her ate each meal in the cell sitting at the table with Mary. The state of Vermont wanted to be sure that Mary did nothing to hurt herself prior to her execution.

The people Mary was allowed to see on a regular basis were the Loukes family, two women guards (Kimball was dismissed by this time), the warden of the prison, the prison chaplain, and because she was Catholic, her priest. There was one other very unusual guest. That guest was Margaret Loukes, the child of the couple who had come to supervise the death watch. Margaret, who was four years-old, was allowed to visit Mary in her cell. Mary showed unusual patience with her young charge, listening as the child rambled as children do so well. The year was 1905, and Margaret would have been almost exactly the same age as the daughter who had slipped from Mary's arms and died.

This time Mary's solitary confinement had been taken to a higher level; the windows of the cell had been painted so that she was prevented from seeing outside.

As bizarre as it may seem, even the gruesome period of awaiting a premature death was becoming routine. Mary spent her last week in a variety of mundane activities. She crocheted lace to be sent to her family and supporters. As remembrances, she made simple children's books to be given to those she had come to know in prison. She wrote notes to her supporters thanking them for their efforts. There were letters allegedly written by Mary that appeared in some newspapers, but the officials of the prison, who monitored her every move, said that these letters were fake.

Whatever term one wanted to use to describe Mary; stoic, emotionless, detached; some felt heartless continued to apply even as she faced death. This time the date of her death was far more real as there were no future legal options open to her.

During the first week of December a story surfaced that Mary was pregnant. Based on the history of her behavior it was not considered an impossibility. After the story appeared in the newspapers, the new prison superintendent, Lovell, and the prison cleric both came forward and denied the story. The prison doctor said he had not seen Mary in months so he could not comment and her priest refused to comment.

Mary's mother and half-sister Catherine came to visit her during the week before the execution. They spent just a half an hour talking with her in the cell. There is no record of what was said or even what emotions were shown. They stayed long enough for Mary's sister to lend her a pair of shoes to be worn to the scaffold.

Local newspapers, that tried to maintain they were neutral, reported that the family's expenses for the trip from Hoosick Falls to Windsor were born by a newspaper in Boston. The Boston newspaper was searching for a sensational story. It would have been a wise move for the newspaper in question; as a mother's final goodbye to a failed daughter was the manner of account that would cut to the heart of many readers. The so-called neutral newspapers said that the tabloid in question had hired a photographer to take pictures of the frail mother and sister.

Who gets to witness the hanging

From the first date in February, there had been a question of who would be permitted to be present when Mary was executed. The newspapers, that had spent so much time and space on the story, wanted witnesses to the final act. The State Attorney General Fitts, who had devoted much of his time to Mary's case, reminded Sheriff Peck that the law required that there be twelve citizens present, one of whom had to be a physician. He suggested strongly that Mary be allowed anyone she wanted as a witness and not to count any clergy that she wanted present. Fitts stressed that the word citizen meant a citizen of Vermont, his point was to exclude the out-of-state press. The implication was clear they had not painted Vermont in a positive light during the period Mary was incarcerated; they should not be present. In the end two reporters, both from Vermont, would witness the execution.

During the final week Mary demonstrated no apprehension about her fate. Her appetite was always good and she slept calmly. She took up reading the Bible.

On one occasion one of her attorneys had her sign a legal document. Speculation began immediately that she was again going to start some form of appeal. The most logical story that surfaced was that the note was an appeal that to the Governor, asking him to stay the execution until after the legislature met in

1906. Eventually the truth came out. The paper was for the insurance company, allowing the benefits of Marcus' life insurance policy to be paid to his brother, William.

Politics

Bell was considered a product of the Republican Party machine. His popularity was rapidly diminishing and he was being challenged by a member of his own party, Percival Clement. With days to go, Clement wrote a letter to Bell asking that Mary's sentence be stayed one more time until after the next session of the legislature.

December 7th

The day before her execution, Mary was visited by both the prison chaplain and her priest. The priest conducted a mass and after he left, Mary assured the matrons that her sins had been forgiven and that she would be "saved." Asked if she was going to confess to the charges against her, Mary had an interesting attitude; she neither denied nor admitted being involved in Marcus' murder. Mary had adopted the attitude that it was not brave to go the gallows and confess; nor would it do her any good to comment on the others who were involved.

Later in the afternoon, Sheriff Peck read Mary the warrant ordering that she suffer "hanging by the neck until she is dead." On the two previous occasions when she had been this close to execution, Mary had heard banging of the gallows being built. This time there were no sounds. All day long she asked if the construction had started, perhaps assuming that there would be yet one more reprieve. As she sat down for her evening meal, the matron told her the scaffold was complete. The hammers had been wrapped in cloth to avoid sounds being heard by Mary or the reporters who had set up camp outside the prison.

The prison superintendent, Lovell, came by in the evening. Mary had always talked longer and more personally with him than with those who were with her each day. She told him that she felt that the lawyers originally assigned to her case had not adequately handled her case. They had let her down and now she would pay the ultimate price. That night she had to be told to go to bed at 11:00.

Lovell reported that he felt that Mary was calm.

December 8th

Governor Bell chose to spend most of his time, between the Supreme Courts decision and the actual execution, in Chicago. He arrived back in Vermont at 3:00 a.m. on December 8th, the day of the execution.

At 8:00 a.m. Bell met with two of Mary's attorneys who maintained they had yet more evidence of insanity. As the lawyers were leaving, Governor Bell informed them that he saw no reason for "further interference." Mary's fate was sealed.

The last day, Mary woke about 5:00 in the morning. She dressed herself and waited. She drank only cold water, choosing to pass on tea and coffee. That morning Mary wrote three last letters. The first two were to her mother and sister. When they were shown to Superintendent Lovell, he said that they were to be mailed as soon as the execution was complete. The third letter, which was to Lovell, was carried in several newspapers. It shows Mary's attitude in her final hours.:

"Mr. Lovell – As I am not much in speaking I pen you a few words as an expression of my extreme gratefulness for your extreme friendness [sic] bestowed upon me since in your care.

Mr. Lovell, I may not always have done as well as I might have done, perhaps, but my only means of statement now for what is past is to tell you that I am sorry and heartily sorry. I know that you have a kind heart and I am bound to think that I may obtain your forgiveness.

You know that Jesus tells us 'If thy brother trespass against thee and turn again to thee saying I repent, forgive him. Be ye tender-hearted forgiving, even as God for Christ's sake as forgiven you in his name'."

The letter was signed Mabel.

When the time came, she passed on her lunch. Her priest came and administered last rites.

At one o'clock, Mary rose and walked unassisted through her cell door. She went down the two flights of stairs that led from the woman's section of the prison to the courtyard where the gallows had been erected. She walked a few steps on the ground then climbed the flight of steps to the gallows. She turned to the hangman and said, "The shoes belong to my sister, please see that she gets them." She stood on the trapdoor; the noose was placed around her neck. Her legs were strapped together. All those who were to witness the execution noted her nerve.

It was reported that Sheriff Peck had developed some illness and felt that the most he could do was stand guard at the door. At 1:13, one of the sheriff's deputies pulled the trapdoor. Mary's neck did not break in the fall and she died of strangulation. At 1:27, the prison doctor declared her dead.

There are two very different reports about what happened when the trapdoor was sprung. The grisly story holds that the prison officials had not allowed for the expansion of the rope and when she dropped Mary toes touched the ground. According to these reports, it was as if she was dancing on her toes until one of the deputies and the doctor who was present pulled on the rope, lifting her feet off the ground. These two men held her suspended for 14 minutes. The other report said that when she first dropped, her toe may have touched the ground but just for just a second. Whichever is the correct, the work of the hangman was done.

Ten minutes before 2:00, the spectacle was all over. Undertaker Louis Haussler, of Hoosick Falls, had loaded Mary's limp body into a coffin. Several guards and trustees carried the coffin to a wagon on which her remains would be taken to a train leaving at 3:00.

Home again

A crowd had gathered in Hoosick Falls to meet Mary's coffin when it was taken from the train. They were disappointed. Not wanting to create a fuss, Haussler had made arrangements for the train to unload Mary's coffin at a special stop out of town.

Mary's funeral was the next morning. The woman who had caused a stir across the country with tens of thousands of signatures raised in her support; the woman whose case was heard by the United States Supreme Court; the woman who had seemed devoid of emotion was buried in St. Mary's Cemetery in the presence of her mother, three sisters, and a few onlookers. She was laid to rest in the family plot.

Marcus Rogers, her victim, was buried in the cemetery just

across the street two years before.

There was no service at the grave and no marker was ever placed on Mary's grave.

What ever happened to

Mary's first attorney, Frank Archibald, was not hurt by Mary accusations about the quality of his service. He went from the State Assembly to the State Senate in 1910. He was appointed Vermont Attorney General from 1918 – 1921

Governor Charles Bell served only the one term during 1904 -06. He died of an apparent heart attack in Grand Central Station in 1909.

Clark C. Fitts served as State Attorney General from 1904-08. He was in the legislature the year Mary's clemency was voted down; born in 1870 he was only 35 at the time of Mary's appeals.

Judge John Watson would become the chief judge of the Vermont Supreme Court

Stella Bates married a man from south of Albany. Her name changed and she was not followed further by the people of Vermont.

Cecilia Blickensderfer would go on to champion other women. Cecelia would be more successful in her home state, where in 1916 she was able to get the sentence of the execution of Amy Archer-Gilligan commuted to life in prison. Amy had killed at least five senior citizens in her charge.